THE CONCISE AACR2

1988 revision

prepared by

Michael Gorman

Chicago: American Library Association
Ottawa: Canadian Library Association   1989
London: The Library Association

Published 1989 by

AMERICAN LIBRARY ASSOCIATION
50 East Huron Street, Chicago, Illinois 60611
ISBN 0-8389-3362-9

CANADIAN LIBRARY ASSOCIATION
200 Elgin Street, Ottawa, Ontario K2P 1L5
ISBN 0-88802-253-0

LIBRARY ASSOCIATION PUBLISHING LIMITED
7 Ridgmount Street, London WC1E 7AE
ISBN 0-85365-799-8

British Library Cataloguing in Publication Data

Gorman, Michael, 1941–
 The concise AACR2. — 1988 revision
 1. Documents. Author cataloguing & descriptive cataloguing
 I. Title II. American Library Association III. Library Association IV. Anglo-American cataloguing rules (2nd ed., 1988 revision)
 025.3′2
 ISBN 0-85365-799-8

Library of Congress Cataloging in Publication Data

Gorman, Michael, 1941–
 The concise AACR2. — 1988 revision
   p.   cm.
 Includes index.
 ISBN 0-8389-3362-9 (alk. paper)
 1. Anglo-American cataloging rules. 2. Descriptive cataloging—Rules. I. Anglo-American cataloguing rules (2nd ed., 1988 revision) II. Title.
 Z694.15.A56G67 1989   89-15110
 025.3′2—dc20   CIP

Contents

JOINT STEERING COMMITTEE FOR REVISION OF AACR

Foreword to 1981 edition

The idea of a concise text of the *Anglo-American Cataloguing Rules* is older than the idea of a second edition of the Rules (*AACR2*) itself. Michael Gorman first began work on what was then thought of as an "abridged edition" of the British Text of AACR 1967 almost two years before the Joint Steering Committee for Revision of AACR (of which I had the privilege to be the first chairperson) was set up to carry out the task of producing *AACR2*.

The principal stimulus to that first project was the need expressed by librarians in third-world countries for a set of basic rules, stated in simple English, that could be used by relatively untrained personnel for relatively small and uncomplicated catalogues; and that would be compatible with a progress to the use of the full *Anglo-American Cataloguing Rules* as staff grew in training and experience and as the catalogues grew in size and complexity. Accordingly, Michael Gorman set to work with a small steering group consisting of Philip K. Escreet and Geoffrey E. Hamilton (both of whom also served later on the Joint Steering Committee for Revision of AACR). Indeed, the project was within sight of completion when he laid it aside to take on a larger task, as one of the two editors of *AACR2*.

One of the main objectives of *AACR2*, attained by its publication in 1978, was to bring together the separate North American and British texts of 1967; and another was to reorganize and express the rules in a simpler and more direct way. So most of the earlier work on the abridgement was nugatory—or, rather, it was used in other ways than originally planned, in *AACR2* itself. However, the Joint Steering Committee soon perceived that the potential was even greater than had previously been estimated for a version of *AACR2* that would meet the needs of the many practitioners and students in our own countries, as well as elsewhere in the world, to whom the full and comprehensive text of *AACR2* tells more than they need to know, or wish to hear, about standards and procedures for catalogue making and the organization of bibliographic records at a particular time in the development of their own libraries, of their own bibliographic services, or of their own studies.

Our main concern was that the quest for simplicity and conciseness in the smaller or less complex library and bibliographic environments should not be impeded by the full text's need to provide in some detail for the whole range of conditions and complexities in the largest or most fully developed libraries and services. We were convinced, too, that the principles and practice set out in *AACR2* were, in general terms, equally valid at both ends of the spectrum of development of library services, and, to change the metaphor, that a clearance of the least familiar trees from the thickly planted wood we call *AACR* would enable everyone who has a need to enter it to see the wood more easily as a whole and to find his or her way through it safely and surely.

These were the aims that led the Joint Steering Committee to seek and obtain approval from its parent bodies, the authors of *AACR2*, for the creation and publication of a concise text, making use of Michael Gorman's dual experience in preparing the earlier abridgement and editing *AACR2*, and of the reconstituted Joint Steering Committee as the authoritative advisory group to ensure the most effective relationship between the concise and the full texts.

These are what the authors now have every confidence and belief has been accomplished in the CONCISE AACR2. It is a high quality working tool of practical value in all kinds of libraries and in many countries, and it embodies the essence of the *Anglo-American Cataloguing Rules* in their most up-to-date form, with all the benefits which that signifies in the wide world of national standards and international harmonization.

PETER R. LEWIS
Director General
Bibliographic Services Division
The British Library

Acknowledgements (1981)

Acknowledgements are due, in the first instance, members of the cataloguing rules committee of the Library Association from 1968 onwards. This shorter edition of the *Anglo-American Cataloguing Rules* has been twelve years in the making. In encouraging me to attempt to produce a standard, though abridged, set of rules, the British cataloguing rules committee is responsible for the present publication in ways which its then members may not be aware. More recently, the Joint Steering Committee for the Revision of AACR (JSC) has given me complete support and encouragement. In particular, I wish to thank Peter Lewis (the chair of JSC from 1976 to 1980), Ronald Hagler, Fran Hinton, and Ben Tucker for their interest, comments, and unfailingly helpful suggestions. Many members of the American Library Association's Catalog Code Revision Committee and, subsequently, Cataloging Committee—Description and Access, have provided me with advice and information.

The following individuals have helped me with comments, criticism, examples, and suggestions: Liz Bishoff, John Byrum, Karen Lunde Christensen, Neal Edgar, Anne Gorman, Eric Hunter, Arnold Wajenberg, Jean Riddle Weihs. My thanks are due my graduate assistants at the University of Illinois (1978–80), Elvira Chavaria and Anne Reuland. Wendy Darre, who typed the many drafts of these rules with her inimitable competence and dispatch, was of invaluable assistance. I am grateful to Helen Cline (managing editor, ALA) for the expertise, care, and hard work that she brought to the task of editing this work for publication. Last, I wish to recognize my daughters, Emma and Alice, without whose unfailing help and encouragement this whole enterprise would have been completed sooner.

MICHAEL GORMAN

Acknowledgements (1989)

I wish to reiterate my gratitude to all those named in the acknowledgements in the first edition of the Concise AACR2. In particular, I am grateful for the continuing help and encouragement of Helen Cline, Ronald Hagler, and Jean Weihs. I would also like to thank my assistants at the University of Illinois (Lisa Boise and Anne Phillips) and my assistant at CSU-Fresno (Janet Bancroft). I wish to express my appreciation to the many teachers of cataloguing that have used the Concise AACR2 in their classes, especially to Ellen Koger who passed on many useful comments. My thanks for many things are due to Karen Schmidt. My special thanks go to Ken Bakewell for all the hard work he has put into compiling the excellent indexes to both editions of this book. My daughters, Emma and Alice, are now grown women of whose accomplishments I am excessively proud. They still think that the editors of cataloguing codes are strange, and who am I to say them nay?

M.G.

General Introduction

This book is intended to convey the essence and basic principles of the second edition of the *Anglo-American cataloguing rules, 1988 revision* (*AACR2R*) without many of that comprehensive work's rules for out-of-the-way and complex materials. Those rules from the full text that have been retained have been rewritten, simplified, and, usually, supplied with new examples. This rewriting is intended to highlight the rules for commonly encountered library materials and to make them even more accessible. Although the method of presentation is different, the end result of the cataloguing process should be the same whether one is using the full or the concise text. In other words, the CONCISE AACR2 prescribes the same cataloguing practice as the full text, but presents only the more generally applicable aspects of that practice and presents them in different terms. The user of the CONCISE AACR2 is referred to the full text for guidance on problems not covered by the concise text and for fuller explanation of rules contained in the concise text. To assist reference between the two texts, a table is given (appendix III) that relates the rules in the concise text to their equivalents in the full text.

The CONCISE AACR2 is intended for cataloguing students, cataloguers in a number of different situations, and other librarians. Persons working in small libraries, especially "one-person" libraries, will be able to do standard cataloguing without the necessity of learning all the details of structure and content of the full text. Beginning students of cataloguing, especially those who wish to learn about cataloguing but not to be cataloguers, will find the CONCISE AACR2 a good introduction to the national cataloguing standard. Paraprofessionals engaged in copy cataloguing by use of catalogue records supplied by national libraries or members of bibliographic networks will find the CONCISE AACR2 an accessible guide to standard cataloguing practice. Public service librarians who wish to understand new developments in descriptive cataloguing practice will find the CONCISE AACR2 a relatively brief summary of that practice. Last, cataloguers working in a non-English language environment will be able to use the CONCISE AACR2 as a readily comprehensible summary of AACR2 practice.

In practical application, the CONCISE AACR2 is likely to be most useful in small general libraries, though it can be used for basic cataloguing in large general libraries and for cataloguing in multimedia resource centres and in nonarchival specialist libraries.

The style and spellings used in the Concise AACR2 follow those of the full text in that they generally follow the *Chicago manual of style*[1] and Webster's *New international dictionary.*[2] Where Webster's permits a British spelling as an alternative, that spelling is followed. As with the full text, care has been taken in the Concise AACR2 to avoid sexist language and sexist implications in the rules and examples.

The order of rules in the Concise AACR2 follows the usual and recommended sequence of cataloguing, in that part 1 deals with the description of the item being catalogued and part 2 deals with the establishment of access points (name headings and uniform titles) to be added to those descriptions, and references to be made to those access points. Separate introductions to part 1 and part 2 begin on pages 5 and 51, respectively.

These rules are based on the idea that one main entry is made for each item described and that this is supplemented by added entries. If, in your catalogue, no distinction is made between main and added entries, use rules 21–29 to decide all the access points to be added to a description and ignore the distinction between main access points and other access points.

Distinguish the headings and/or uniform titles added to the description by giving them on separate lines above the description. If any entry begins with a title proper (that is, the first element of the description—see rule 1B), give the description alone *or* repeat the title proper on a line above the description.

Example of entry with heading:

```
Brodie, Fawn M.
  The devil drives : a life of Sir Richard
  Burton / Fawn M. Brodie. -- Penguin, 1971. --
  505 p. -- ISBN 0-14-003323-8
```

Example of one style of entry under title proper:

```
  The American heritage dictionary of the
  English language. -- Paperback ed. / Peter
  Davies, editor. -- Dell, 1970. -- 820 p. --
  ISBN 0-440-10207-3
```

---

1. The Chicago manual of style : for authors, editors and copywriters. — 13th ed., rev. and expanded. — Chicago ; London : University of Chicago Press, 1982.

2. Webster's third new international dictionary of the English language, unabridged. — Springfield Mass. : Merriam-Webster ; Harlow, Essex : Distributed by Longman Group, c1986.

Some rules or parts of rules are designated as *optional*, or are introduced by the word *optionally*, or are presented as an *either/or* choice. Decide which option is to be used and in which circumstances. Base your decision on your judgement of what is best for your catalogue and its users. Make a record of such decisions.

Sometimes a cataloguer needs to exercise judgement and decide on an interpretation. The need for these is indicated in the CONCISE AACR2 by words and phrases such as *if appropriate, important*, and *if necessary*. Apply judgements and interpretations consistently within one catalogue, and, when possible, record each exercise of judgement.

Rules on capitalization and a glossary are given as appendices I and II.

The examples used throughout the CONCISE AACR2 have been chosen to illustrate commonly encountered cases. Examples drawn from a variety of media and from modern English-language items have been preferred. Remember that examples only illustrate the rules and are not intended to expand on the rules unless a rule specifically says so. The existence of a spaced-out mark of omission (. . .) in an example indicates that the example is incomplete; the usual mark of omission (...) is one intended to form part of the entry.

PART 1 # Description

Introduction

This part of the CONCISE AACR2 contains instructions on how to make a description of an item that has been acquired by your library. This description is displayed in a catalogue at one or more access points established for the item according to the instructions in part 2 (pages 51 to 129).

The rules are based on those in part I of the full text of *AACR2*. In the CONCISE AACR2 only the usual case is dealt with. For more difficult materials or for out-of-the-way problems, see the full text.

Instead of the analytical structure of part I of *AACR2* in which each type of library material is dealt with separately as far as description is concerned, the CONCISE AACR2 deals with all materials in one chapter. Thus, all the rules on physical description, for example, will be found on pages 29–37.

In describing library materials according to these rules, a basic principle is that you describe what you have in hand. For example, a manuscript reproduced as a book is described as a book; a book reproduced on microfilm is described as a microfilm. Do not describe what something was; describe what something is.

The generalizing of the descriptive rules in the CONCISE AACR2 has led to the loss of some nuances of the original text. None of these nuances affects access to the descriptions. For example, the rules on sources of information in this text may lead to a diminished use of square brackets in the entry. This small loss of a few refinements will not affect the user of a catalogue in which CONCISE AACR2 entries are found.

Not all the elements set out for the description of materials will be needed for a particular item or for a particular catalogue. See rule 0E for a specification of the minimum elements needed. In particular any detail described as *optional* need not necessarily be included in a description. Most notes (see rule 7) are optional; a note should only be made if it is necessary to the understanding or identification of the item being described, *or* if rule 7 indicates that it is required.

Some measurements prescribed in rule 5D are not metric. Use metric measurements in their place if they are more suitable for the material or the country in which the cataloguing is being done.

If you are cataloguing in a non–English-speaking country or region, substitute your language or your language abbreviations for the English terms or abbreviations specified in these rules. However, do not translate data transcribed from the item being catalogued.

The Description of Library Materials

Contents

8.   STANDARD NUMBER
8A.   Preliminary rule
8A1. Punctuation
8B.   Standard number

9.   SUPPLEMENTARY ITEMS

10.   ITEMS MADE UP OF MORE THAN ONE TYPE OF
        MATERIAL

11.   FACSIMILES, PHOTOCOPIES, AND OTHER
        REPRODUCTIONS

0. GENERAL RULE

0A. Sources of information

Most items acquired by a library belong to one of the following types of publication. For each type the chief source of information is:

TYPE OF MATERIAL	CHIEF SOURCE OF INFORMATION
Books, pamphlets, and other printed texts	Title page
Computer files	Title screen
Graphic materials (pictures, posters, wallcharts, etc.)	The item itself
Maps and other cartographic materials	The item itself
Microforms	Title frame
Motion pictures and video-recordings	The item itself
Printed music	Title page
Sound recordings	
Discs	The label (if two, both taken together)
Tapes	The item itself and its label(s)
Three-dimensional objects (models, dioramas, games, etc.)	The object itself

The chief source for a *serial item* is the chief source of the first issue, or in its absence, the earliest available issue.[1]

Use information found in the chief source in preference to information found elsewhere. If the necessary information cannot be found in the chief source, take it from:

    1) any other source that is part of the item

or

    2) any other source that accompanies the item and was issued by the publisher or issuer of that item (for example, a container, a printed insert).

If all else fails, take the information from any available source (for example, a reference work) *or* compose it yourself.

If you have taken the information from outside the item *or* have composed it yourself, enclose it in square brackets and indicate the source in a note (see rule 7B5).

0B. Items with several chief sources of information

0B1. Single part items. If an item is in one physical piece abut has more than one chief source of information, choose the chief source according to the following rules.

    a) Use the chief source of information with the latest date of publication.

    b) If one chief source treats the item as a single item and the other as part of a multipart item, use the source that corresponds to the way in which the item is being catalogued (for example, use the multipart item source if you are describing all the parts in one description).

    c) If the item contains words (written, spoken, or sung) all in one language, use the source in the language of the item (for example, use an English title page for a book in English).

    d) If the item is in a number of languages, use the source in the language occurring first in the following list: English, the first occurring source in any other language using the roman alphabet, the first occurring source in any other language.

---

1. The chief source for a printed serial that has no title page is (in this order of preference):

a) the title page for part of the serial	e) the editorial pages
b) the cover	f) the colophon
c) the caption	g) other pages
d) the masthead	

0B2. Multipart items (for example, a serial). If an item is in a number of physically separate pieces, use the chief source for the first piece. If there is no first piece, use the chief source that gives the most information. If the information differs in the chief sources of the other pieces, and if the difference is important, make a note (see rule 7B5).

0C. The description
The description is divided into the following areas:

> title and statement of responsibility
> edition
> special area (*only for* serials; computer files; maps, etc.; music)
> publication, etc.
> physical description
> series
> notes (*a repeatable area*)
> standard number and terms of availability.

0D. Punctuation of the description
Separate the areas listed in rule 0C by using one of the following methods. *Either* introduce each area (except the first) by a full stop, space, dash, space (. —) as set out here:

```
Title and statement of responsibility. --
Edition. -- Special area. -- Publication, etc. --
Physical description. -- Series. -- Note. --
Note. -- Standard number and terms of
availability
```

or begin a new paragraph for certain areas as set out here:

```
Title and statement of responsibility. --
Edition. -- Special area. -- Publication,
etc.
Physical description. -- Series
Notes (each note occupies a separate
paragraph, though notes may be combined
(see rule 7A1))
Standard number and terms of availability
```

Within each area, introduce each element (a part of an area), except the first, by special punctuation as set out at the head of the rules in this part for that area (1A1, 2A1, etc.).

Omit any area or element that does not apply to the item being catalogued. Omit also its introductory punctuation.

Here are two examples of simple descriptions (one for a book, one for a sound disc). Each is set out in both the ways specified above.

Example 1. First layout

```
The fair garden and the swarm of beasts :
the library and the young adult / Margaret
A. Edwards. -- Rev. and expanded [ed.]. --
New York : Hawthorn, c1974. -- 194 p. ; 22
cm. -- Previous ed. 1969
```

Example 1. Second layout

```
    The fair garden and the swarm of beasts :
the library and the young adult / Margaret
A. Edwards. -- Rev. and expanded [ed.]. --
New York : Hawthorn, c1974
    194 p. ; 22 cm.
    Previous ed. 1969
```

Example 2. First layout

```
A night on the town [sound recording] / Rod
Stewart. -- London : Riva Records :
Distributed by WEA Records, 1976. -- 1 sound
disc (39 min.) : analog, 33 1/3 rpm,
stereo. ; 12 in.
```

Example 2. Second layout

```
    A night on the town [sound recording] /
Rod Stewart. -- London : Riva Records :
Distributed by WEA Records, 1976
    1 sound disc (39 min.) : analog, 33 1/3
rpm, stereo. ; 12 in.
```

0E. Levels of detail in the description

As a basic minimum, include *at least* the areas and elements (provided that they apply to the item) set out in this illustration:

```
Title proper / first statement of
responsibility². -- Edition statement. --
Special area for serials, computer files,
maps. -- First named publisher, etc., date. --
Extent of item. -- Required note(s). --
Standard number
```

Include further information as set out in rules 1–8 when appropriate for your catalogue or your library.

1. TITLE AND STATEMENT OF RESPONSIBILITY AREA

Contents:
   1A. Preliminary rule
   1B. Title proper
   1C. General material designation
   1D. Parallel titles
   1E. Other title information
   1F. Statements of responsibility
   1G. Items without a collective title

1A. Preliminary rule

1A1. Punctuation
Precede the title of a separate part, supplement, or section by a full stop, space (.).

Enclose the general material designation in square brackets ([]).

Precede a parallel title by a space, equals sign, space (=).

Precede other title information by a space, colon, space (:).

Precede the first statement of responsibility by a space, diagonal slash, space (/).

Precede each other statement of responsibility by a space, semicolon, space (;).

1B. Title proper

1B1. Transcribe the title proper exactly as it is found in the chief source of information except that the punctuation and the capitalization found there need not be followed. See appendix I for rules on capitalization.

---

2. If the person or body named in this statement is recognizably the same as that chosen for the main entry heading (see rules 23–28) and the rest of the statement consists only of the word "by" (or its equivalent in another language), omit the statement.

Gone with the wind

The big money

White mansions

McAuslan in the rough and other stories

16 greatest original bluegrass hits

The 4:50 from Paddington

The Fresno bee

Index to the Columbia edition of the works
of John Milton

Son of the black stallion

Elvis is dead, & I'm not feeling too good
myself

Les amants

1B2. If the name of an author, publisher, etc., is an integral part of the title proper, record it as such. Do not repeat the name in a statement of responsibility (see rule 1F1).

The Rolling Stones' greatest hits

The most of P.G. Wodehouse

The complete Firbank

Geographia A1 road atlas of London

The New Oxford book of English verse

When hearts are trumps by Tom Hall / Will H.
Bradley
(*a poster by Bradley advertising a play by Hall*)

Proceedings of the Annual Workshop on
School Libraries

1B3. If the title proper consists solely of the name of the person or body responsible for the item, give that name as the title proper.

Byron
(*a book of poems*)

14

```
Waylon Jennings
```
(*a sound recording of performances by Jennings*)

```
International Conference on the Law of
the Sea
```
(*proceedings of the conference*)

1B4. If the item being catalogued is a part of a larger publication (for example, a volume of a multivolume set, a disc that is part of a set of discs, a serial that is a continuing part of another larger serial)
or is a supplement to another publication
and the title proper consists of the title of the larger publication and an indication of the part or supplement
and the two parts of the title are not linked grammatically,
give the title proper as the title of the larger work followed by the indication of the part.

```
Faust. Part 1
```

```
Stocks & bonds today. Supplement
```

```
The music of the masters. 1850-1889
```


1B5. If the title proper of a serial includes a date or numbering that varies from issue to issue, omit this date or numbering. Indicate the omission by " ... " unless the date or numbering occurs at the beginning of the title.

```
Report on the ... Conference on AIDS and
Alternative Medicine
```
        (*chief source reads:* Report on the Second Conference on AIDS and Alternative Medicine)

but   ```Annual report```

not   ```... annual report```
        (*chief source reads:* 1987 Annual Report)

1B6. If there is no chief source of information (for example, a book without a title page; a computer file without a title screen), supply a title proper from the rest of the item or from elsewhere (for example, a reference source).

If no title can be found anywhere, make up a brief descriptive title yourself. Give a supplied or made-up title in square brackets and make a note (see rule 7B5).

[Map of Australia] .

[Photograph of Kenneth Williams]

1B7. If the title appears in two or more languages, use the one that is in the main language of the item as the title proper. If there is more than one main language, use the title that appears first.

1C. General material designation. *Optional addition*

1C1. General rule. If you want to use a general material designation as an "early warning" to the catalogue user, give a term from the following list immediately following the title proper.[3]

art original	globe	picture
art reproduction	kit	realia
braille	manuscript	slide
chart (*not a map*)	map	sound recording
computer file	microform	technical drawing
diorama	microscope slide	toy
filmstrip	model	transparency
flash card	motion picture	videorecording
game	music	

 WordPerfect [computer file]

 The San Joaquin Valley [diorama]

 Exploring the human body [kit]

 The New York times [microform]

 Black and blue [sound recording]

For material for the blind and visually impaired, add "(braille)", "(large print)", or "(tactile)" to any of the above terms when appropriate.

 The banks of green willow [music (braille)]

 Camden [map (large print)]

1C2. If the item is a reproduction of an item in another form (for example, a book in microform; a map on a slide), give the general material

---

3. This list reflects North American practice as set out in AACR2, 1988 revision, rule 1.1C.

designation appropriate to the reproduction (for example, in the case of a map on a slide, give "[slide]").

1C3. Because they are *optional*, general material designations are not given in the rest of the examples in this part (other than in rule 10C). Do not take this as implying that they should or should not be used in a particular case.

1D. Parallel titles
If the title appears in the chief source of information in two or more languages, choose one of these as the title proper (see rule 1B7). Give one other title (the one appearing first or the one following the title proper) as the parallel title.

> Dansk-Engelske ordbog = Danish-English dictionary

> Road map of France = Carte routière de la France

1E. Other title information

1E1. Transcribe other title information (for example, a subtitle) appearing in the chief source of information.

> Bits of paradise : twenty-one uncollected stories

> Aspects of Alice : Lewis Carroll's dreamchild as seen through the critics' looking-glasses, 1865-1971

> Annie Hall : a nervous romance

1E2. If there is more than one subtitle (or unit of other title information) appearing in the chief source of information, give them in the order in which they appear there.

> Clawhammer banjo : the return of the clawhammer banjo : twenty Irish, English, and American tunes

1E3. If the other title information is lengthy and does not contain important information, omit it.

1E4. If the title proper needs explanation, make a brief addition as other title information.

>   Shelley : [selections]

>   Conference on Aesthetic Values and the
>   Ideal : [proceedings]

1F. Statements of responsibility

1F1. First statement of responsibility. Always give the statement of responsibility that appears first in the chief source of information, unless the name of the author, publisher, etc., has already appeared as part of the title (see rule 1B2).

>   Hangover Square / by Patrick Hamilton

>   Cruising / Jonathan Raban

>   Honky tonk heroes / Waylon Jennings

>   Shoot low, lads, they're ridin' Shetland
>   ponies / Lewis Grizzard

>   Proceedings / International Conference on
>   Nematodes

>   The monocled mutineer / William Allison and
>   John Fairley

>   American literature : a representative
>   anthology of American writing from colonial
>   times to the present / selected and
>   introduced by Geoffrey Moore

but   The portable Oscar Wilde

not   The portable Oscar Wilde / Oscar Wilde

1F2. Other statements of responsibility. Give other statements of responsibility that appear in the chief source of information in the form and order in which they appear there. If the order is ambiguous, give them in the order that makes the most sense.

>   Snow White and the seven dwarfs : a tale
>   from the Brothers Grimm / translated by
>   Randall Jarrell ; pictures by Nancy Ekholm
>   Burkert

18

```
Plats du jour / Patience Gray and Primrose
Boyd ; illustrated by David Gentleman
```

```
Dougal and the blue cat : original
soundtrack of the Nat Cohen-EMI film /
original story written and directed by Serge
Danot ; English version by Eric Thompson ;
music by Joss Baselli
```

1F3. Give the statements of responsibility after the title information even if they appear before the title in the chief source of information.

```
Only the lonely / Roy Orbison
```
(disc label reads: ROY ORBISON
Only The Lonely)

1F4. If no statement of responsibility appears in the chief source of information, do not supply one. If such a statement is necessary to make the description complete, give it in a note (see rule 7B6).

1F5. If a single statement of responsibility names more than three persons or bodies, omit all but the first named. Indicate the omission by " ... " and add "et al." in square brackets.

```
London consequences : a novel / edited by
Margaret Drabble and B.S. Johnson ; the work
also of Paul Ableman ... [et al.]
```
(second statement names fifteen other persons)

1F6. Omit statements of responsibility relating to persons or bodies with minor responsibility for the item. Such minor responsibility includes:

> writing an introduction to a book
> performing "serious" music or recorded speech (see also rule 7B6)
> performing in a motion picture (see also rule 7B6)
> playing a subsidiary role in producing a motion picture (for example, assistant director, make-up artist, editor)
> being responsible for the physical production of the item.

1F7. Omit titles, qualifications, etc., attached to personal names in statements of responsibility unless omitting them makes the statement unintelligible or misleading.

The larks of Surinam / by Robert Antrobus
  (*name appears as:* Dr. Robert Antrobus)

Koalas : our friends from Down Under / by
S.K. Arline
  (*name appears as:* S.K. Arline, F.R.N.Z.S.)

but

The prisoner of Chillon / Lord Byron

Fruitful and responsible love / Pope John
Paul II

Horton hears a Who! / by Dr. Seuss

1F8. Add a word or phrase to the statement of responsibility only if it is necessary to make the statement clear.

Denmark : a film / [produced and directed
by] Eigil Andersen

The best man / Tomi Ungerer ; [designed by]
Bob Cox

but

Red headed stranger / Willie Nelson

Catalogue / Liverpool Public Library

1G. Items without a collective title

1G1. With predominant part. If an item contains two or more separately titled parts *and* lacks a collective title, make a single description if one of the parts is predominant. Use the title of that part as the title proper and name the other parts in a note. When appropriate, make added entries for the other parts.

Piano concerto no. 27 in B flat, K595 /
  Mozart
Note: Overtures to Così fan tutte, The
  impresario, The magic flute, and Don Giovanni
  on side 2

1G2. Without predominant part. If no one part predominates:
either make a separate entry for each part (see also rule 7B16)

20

or give all the titles in the order in which they appear in the chief source *and* make added entries for all the parts other than the first named as instructed in rule 29B8.

If you are making one entry for the item and all the parts are by the same person(s) or body (bodies), separate the titles by a space, semicolon, space (;).

> The Brandenburg concertos no. 2 & no. 6 ;
> The clavier concerto in D minor / Bach

If you are making one entry for the item and the parts are by different persons or bodies, give the titles and statements of responsibility in the order in which they appear in the chief source. Separate the titles and statements of responsibility of one part from those of another by a full stop followed by two spaces (.).

> Rosaceae : twelve hand-coloured etchings /
> by Fenella Wingift. Liliaceae : twelve hand-
> coloured etchings / by Pandora Braithwaite

2. EDITION AREA

Contents:
    2A. Preliminary rule
    2B. Edition statement
    2C. Statements of responsibility relating to the edition

2A. Preliminary rule

2A1. Punctuation
Precede this area by a full stop, space, dash, space (. —).
Precede a statement of responsibility following an edition statement by a space, diagonal slash, space (/).

2A2. Take information for this area from the chief source of information (see rule 0A) *or* from any formal statement made by the publisher or issuer of the item either on the item or in material which accompanies the item (for example, a container, a record sleeve).

Enclose information taken from anywhere else in square brackets.

2B. Edition statement
Give the edition statement as found *except:*

1) replace words with standard abbreviations
and

2) replace words with numbers where appropriate.

> New ed.
> (*appears in item as:* New Edition)

> Rev. ed.
> (*appears in item as:* Revised edition)

> 3rd ed.
> (*appears in item as:* Third edition)

> TryoPoly. -- Chicago ed.
> (*a game with different versions for different cities*)

> The international herald-tribune. --
> Airmail ed.

2C. Statements of responsibility relating to the edition

2C1. If a statement of responsibility relates to one or some editions but not to all, give it after the edition statement if there is one. Follow the rules in 1F.

> A dictionary of modern English usage / by
> H.W. Fowler. -- 2nd ed. / revised by Ernest
> Gowers

> Anglo-American cataloguing rules. -- 2nd
> ed. / prepared by the American Library
> Association ... [et al.] ; edited by Michael
> Gorman and Paul W. Winkler

2C2. If there is no edition statement, give such a statement of responsibility in the title and statement of responsibility area.

> Little Dorrit / Charles Dickens ; edited by
> John Holloway

> From Atlanta to the sea / William T.
> Sherman ; edited with an introduction by B.H.
> Liddell Hart

2C3. If there is doubt about whether a statement of responsibility applies to all editions or only to some, give it in the title and statement of responsibility area.

22

3. SPECIAL AREA FOR SERIALS, COMPUTER FILES, MAPS AND OTHER CARTOGRAPHIC MATERIALS, AND MUSIC

3A. Serials

3A1. Punctuation

Precede this area by a full stop, space, dash, space (. —).

Follow the designation and/or date of the first issue by a hyphen and four spaces (-).

Enclose a date following the designation of the first issue in parentheses (()).

Precede a new series of numbering, etc., by a space, semicolon, space (;).

3A2. Designation of first issue. Give the designation (volume, part, numbering, etc.) of the first issue of a serial. Replace words with standard abbreviations. Replace words with numbers where appropriate.

```
Inside sports. -- Vol. 1, no. 1-

Private eye. -- No. 1-
```

3A3. Date. If the first issue of a serial is designated only by a date, give that date. Replace words with standard abbreviations. Replace words with numbers where appropriate.

```
Master's theses in education. -- 1951-
```

If the first issue is identified by both numbering, etc., and a date, give the numbering, etc., before the date.

```
Terrapin & turtle world. -- Vol. 1, no. 1
(spring 1977)-
```

3A4. No designation. If the first issue lacks a designation or date, give "[No. 1]- ". If, however, later issues adopt a numbering, follow that.

```
[Pt. 1]-
```
(later issues numbered: Part 2, Part 3, *etc.)*

3A5. Completed serials. If the serial is completed, give the designation and/or date of the first issue followed by the designation and/or date of the last issue.

```
Quarter horse newsletter. -- No. 1 (May
1973)-no. 17 (Sept. 1974)
```

23

3A6. Successive designations. If a serial starts a new system of designation without changing its title, give the designation of the first and last issues under the old system, followed by the designation of the first issue under the new system.

```
Language/art/language. -- Vol. 1, no. 1-vol.
3, no. 7 ; no. 32-
```

3A7. More than one system of designation. If a serial has more than one separate system of designation, give each in the order in which it appears in the chief source of information. Separate the designations by four spaces, equals sign, space (=) *or*, if the serial is completed, by a space, equals sign, space (=).

```
English review. -- Vol. 1, no. 1-    = no. 11-
```

3A8. New serial. If the title proper of a serial changes (see rule 22C), make a new description and close the old description (see rule 3A5).

3B. Computer files

3B1. Punctuation
Precede this area by a full stop, space, dash, space (. --).

3B2. File designation. If the information is readily available, name the type of file. Use one of the following terms:

```
computer data
computer program(s)
computer data and program(s).
```

```
The 1988 U.S. general election,
demographics. -- Computer data
```

```
Reference desk staffing / Gunnar Larsen. --
Computer program
```

```
TorQuiz. -- Computer data and program
```

Optionally, if you have used the general material designation "computer file", omit "computer" from the file designation.

```
Reference desk staffing [computer file] /
Gunnar Larsen. -- Program
```

3C. Maps and other cartographic materials

3C1. Punctuation
Precede this area by a full stop, space, dash, space (. —).
Precede a projection statement by a space, semicolon, space (;).

3C2. Scale. Give the scale of a cartographic item if it is found on the item or if it can be determined easily (for example, from a bar graph). Give the scale as a representative fraction.[4]
Precede the scale by "Scale".

> Scale 1:500,000

> Scale 1:63,360
> (*appears on item as:* One inch to a mile)

If the scale appears as a representative fraction and in words, give the representative fraction only.

> Scale 1:253,440
> (*also appears as:* One inch to four miles)

If the scale does not appear on the item and cannot easily be determined, do not give a scale statement.

If the description is of a multipart item with two or more scales, give the statement "Scales vary".

3C3. Projection. Give the statement of projection if it is found on the item. Replace words with standard abbreviations.

> Transverse Mercator proj.
> (*no scale given on item*)

3D. Music (Scores, etc.)

3D1. Punctuation
Precede this area by a full stop, space, dash, space (. —).

3D2. Musical presentation statement. If a statement indicating the physical presentation of the music appears separately in the chief source of

---

4. 1/2 in. to a mile = 1:126,720   2 in. to a mile = 1:31,680
     1 in. to a mile = 1:63,360   4 in. to a mile = 1:15,840
If the scale is given in centimetres (cm.) to kilometres (km.), multiply the km. by 100,000. For example, 1 cm. to 2.5 km. equals 1:250,000 as a representative fraction.

information, give it here. Typical musical presentation statements include "Miniature score", "playing score", and "Full score".

```
Symphony in B flat for concert band /
Hindemith. -- Miniature score
```

4. PUBLICATION, DISTRIBUTION, ETC., AREA

Contents:
- 4A.   Preliminary rule
- 4B.   General rule
- 4C.   Place of publication, distribution, etc.
- 4D.   Name of publisher, distributor, etc.
- 4E.   Date of publication, distribution, etc.

4A. Preliminary rule

4A1. Punctuation
Precede this area by a full stop, space, dash, space (. —).
Precede a second place of publication, etc., by a space, semicolon, space (;).
Precede the name of a publisher, etc., by a space, colon, space (:).
Precede the date of publication, etc., by a comma, space (,).

4A2. Take information for this area from the chief source of information (see rule 0A) or from any formal statement made by the publisher or issuer of the item either on the item or in material accompanying the item (for example, a container, a record sleeve). Enclose information taken from anywhere else in square brackets.

4B. General rule

4B1. In this area, give information relating to the publisher, distributor, etc., of the item and the date of its publication, distribution, etc.

4B2. If an item has two or more places of publication, distribution, etc., *and/or* two or more publishers, distributors, etc., give the first named place and publisher, distributor, etc. If another place and publisher, distributor, etc., is more prominent in the chief source of information, also give that place and publisher, distributor, etc.

If a place and/or publisher, distributor, etc., in your country is named in a secondary position, *optionally* add that place and publisher, distributor, etc.

> New York : Dutton ; Toronto : Clarke, Irwin
> (*if you are cataloguing in Canada*)

> Burbank, Calif. : Warner Bros. ; London : Butterfly Records
> (*if you are cataloguing in the United Kingdom*)

4C. Place of publication, distribution, etc.

4C1. Give the place of publication as it appears on the item.

> London

> Los Angeles

> Tolworth, England

4C2. If a publisher, distributor, etc., has offices in more than one place, always give the first named place. *Optionally*, give any other place that is in your country. Omit all other places.

> New York ; London
> (*if you are cataloguing in the United Kingdom*)

> London ; Melbourne
> (*if you are cataloguing in Australia*)

> London ; New York
> (*if you are cataloguing in the United States*)

4C3. If the place of publication, distribution, etc., is uncertain or unknown, leave out this element.

4D. Name of publisher, distributor, etc.

4D1. Give the name of the publisher, distributor, etc., in the shortest form in which it can be understood and identified. Omit accompanying wording that implies the publishing function.

> London : MacGibbon & Kee

> Berkeley : Kicking Mule Records

```
       London  :  Cape
not    London  :  Jonathan Cape

       London  :  Allen & Unwin
not    London  :  Published by Allen & Unwin

but    London  :  W.H. Allen
not    London  :  Allen
```
        (avoids confusion with other publishers called Allen)

4D2. If the name of the publisher, etc., appears in a recognizable form in a preceding area, give it here in a shortened form.

```
       Smallpox / World Health Organization. --
       Geneva : WHO
```

4D3. If the name of the publisher, etc., is unknown, leave out this element.

4D4. If the person or body named here is a distributor, *optionally* add "distributor" in square brackets.

```
       London : Rousseur [distributor]
```

4E. Date of publication, distribution, etc.

4E1. Give the year of publication, distribution, etc., of the edition named in the edition area (see rule 2B). Ignore dates of later issues of the same edition. If there is no edition statement, give the year of first publication of the item in hand. Give the year in arabic numbers.

```
       Ottawa : Canadian Library Association, 1985
```

4E2. If no date of publication is found on the item, give (in this order of preference):

a) the year of publication found on material accompanying the item

```
       London : Virgin, 1985
       (found on record sleeve)
```

b) the latest copyright year found on the item, preceded by "c" or, for some sound recordings, "p"

```
       New York : Knopf, c1954

       New York : Polydor, p1979
```

28

c) an approximate year preceded by "ca." and enclosed in square brackets.

> Toronto : Scaramouche, [ca. 1950]
> (*no date found but probably around 1950*)

5. PHYSICAL DESCRIPTION AREA

Contents:
  5A. Preliminary rule
  5B. Extent of item
  5C. Other physical details
  5D. Dimensions
  5E. Accompanying material

5A. Preliminary rule

5A1. Punctuation
Precede this area by a full stop, space, dash, space (. —) *or* start a new paragraph (see rule 0D).

Precede the other physical details (i.e., other than extent or dimensions) by a space, colon, space (:).

Precede the dimensions by a space, semicolon, space (;).

Precede the statement of accompanying materials by a space, plus sign, space (+).

5A2. Source of information. Take information for this area from any source, but prefer information taken from the item itself.

5B. Extent of item

5B1. Items other than books and atlases. Record the number of parts of an item by giving the number of pieces, etc., in arabic numbers and the name of the item or parts taken from the following list.

a) *Art pictures.* Use "art original", "art print", or "art reproduction", as appropriate.

> 3 art prints

> 1 art reproduction

b) *Charts, etc.* Use "chart", "poster", "flip chart", or "wall chart", as appropriate.

> 3 charts

> 2 posters

c) *Computer files.* Use "computer cartridge", "computer cassette", "computer disk", or "computer reel", as appropriate.

> 1 computer disk

Optionally, if you have used the general material designation "computer file", omit "computer" from the statement of extent.

> 1 disk

d) *Filmstrips and filmslips.* Use "filmstrip" or "filmslip", as appropriate.

> 1 filmstrip

e) *Maps, globes.* Use "map" or "globe", as appropriate.

> 3 maps

> 1 globe

f) *Microforms.* Use "microfiche", "microfiche cassette", or "microfilm", as appropriate. Add "cartridge", "cassette", or "reel", as appropriate, to "microfilm".

> 7 microfiches

> 1 microfilm reel

Optionally, if you have used the general material designation "microform", omit "micro" from the statement of extent.

> 7 fiches

> 1 film reel

g) *Motion pictures.* Use "film cartridge", "film cassette", "film loop", or "film reel", as appropriate.

> 4 film reels

Optionally, if you have used the general material designation "motion picture", omit "film" from the statement of extent.

> 4 reels

h) *Music.* Use "score" or "part", as appropriate.

       1 score

       2 parts

i) *Slides.* Use "slide".

       3 slides

j) *Sound recordings.* Use "sound cartridge", "sound cassette", "sound disc", or "sound tape reel", as appropriate.

       2 sound cassettes

Optionally, if you have used the general material designation "sound recording", omit "sound" from the statement of extent.

       2 cassettes

k) *Three-dimensional objects.* Use an appropriate term (for example, "diorama", "game", "model").

       1 diorama

       2 jigsaw puzzles

       1 paperweight

l) *Videorecordings.* Use "videocartridge", "videocassette", "videodisc", or "videoreel", as appropriate.

       1 videodisc

Optionally, if you have used the general material designation "videorecording", omit "video" from the statement of extent.

       1 disc

m) *Graphic materials other than those specified above.* Use an appropriate term (for example, "flash card", "photograph").

       3 photographs

       1 technical drawing

       2 pictures

If the item being described has a playing time that is stated on the item *or* that can be ascertained easily, add the playing time in parentheses.

```
1 sound disc (35 min.)

2 videoreels (88 min.)

8 film reels (105 min.)

5 sound cassettes (30 min. each)
```

5B2. Extent of books, atlases, and other printed items. Single volumes.
Record the number of pages in the main numbered sequence.

```
327 p.
```

If there is more than one main numbered sequence, give the number of pages in each sequence in the order in which the sequences appear in the item.

```
320, 200 p.
```

Ignore unnumbered sequences and minor sequences.

```
327 p.   not   [32], 327 p.

119 p.   not   xii, 119 p.

300 p.   not   12, 300 p.
```

If there are no numbered sequences or a great many numbered sequences, give "1 v.".

5B3. Extent of books, atlases, and other printed items. More than one volume (including completed printed serials). Record the number of volumes in a multivolume book or in a "dead"[5] printed serial.

```
3 v.

200 v.

19 v.
```

5B4. Incomplete items. If a multipart item is incomplete or if the item being described is a "live"[6] serial, give one of the terms listed in 5B1 or "v." (for printed materials) preceded by three spaces.

---

5. A serial that is completed.

6. A serial that is still being issued.

```
maps

film reels

v.
```

5C. Other physical details

Give other physical details as set out here.

1) *Books, music, microforms, and printed serials.* If the item contains illustrations, give "ill.". If the illustrations are numbered sequentially, give the number in arabic numerals.

```
320 p. : ill.

320 p. : 37 ill.

1 score : ill.

3 microfiches : ill.
```

If all the illustrations are coloured, give "col. ill.". If some of the illustrations are coloured, give "ill. (some col.)".

```
320 p. : col. ill.

320 p. : 30 col. ill.

320 p. : 130 ill. (some col.)
```

2) *Computer files.* If the file is programmed so that the textual and/or graphic data displays in colour, give "col.". If the file has integral sound, give "sd.".

```
1 computer disk : col., sd.
```

3) *Graphic items (two-dimensional).* If the item is coloured, give "col.".

```
3 filmstrips : col.

7 posters : col.
```

If a filmstrip or slide set has integral sound, give "sd.".

```
3 filmstrips : col., sd.

48 slides : col., sd.
```

If, however, a sound recording merely accompanies the filmstrip or slide set, treat it as accompanying material (see rule 5E) or, if appropriate, as a kit (see rule 10C).

4) *Maps, globes.* If the map or globe is coloured, give "col.".

>   1 globe : col.

>   3 maps : col.

5) *Motion pictures and videorecordings.* Indicate whether the motion picture or videorecording is sound or silent by giving "sd." or "si.".

>   1 film reel (30 min.) : si.

>   1 videodisc (14 min.) : sd.

If the item is coloured, give "col.".

>   14 film reels : sd., col.

6) *Sound recordings.* For analog discs, give "analog" and the playing speed in revolutions per minute (rpm).

>   2 sound discs : analog, 33 1/3 rpm

For all other sound recordings, give "analog" or "digital",[7] as appropriate.

>   2 sound discs : digital

>   2 sound cassettes : analog

For all sound recordings, give the number of sound channels if the information is readily available. Use one of the following terms.

mono. (*for monaural recordings*)
stereo. (*for stereophonic recordings*)
quad. (*for quadraphonic recordings*)

>   2 sound cassettes : analog, stereo.

>   1 sound disc (30 min.) : analog, 33 1/3 rpm,
>   stereo.

7) *Three-dimensional objects.* Give the material(s) of which the object is made, unless the materials are numerous or unknown.

>   2 paperweights : glass

>   1 diorama : papier mâché

>   1 game : wood & plastic

---

7. A digital recording is one in which the sound is digitally encoded on the item (for example, a "compact disc").

34

If the object is black and white, give "b&w". If the object is in one or two colours, give the name(s) of the colour(s). If it is in three or more colours, give "col.".

```
1 box : wood & metal, b&w

1 vase : porcelain, blue & white

1 paperweight : glass, col.
```

5D. Dimensions

Give the dimensions of the item as set out here.

1) *Books, pamphlets, and other printed texts; music; and printed serials.* Give the outside height in centimetres (cm.) to the next centimetre up.

```
325 p. : ill. ; 27 cm.

3 v. : col. ill. ; 25 cm.

1 score ; 24 cm.
```

2) *Filmstrips and filmslips.* Give the gauge (width) in millimetres (mm.).

```
1 filmstrip : col. ; 35 mm.
```

3) *Globes.* Give the diameter of the globe in centimetres.

```
1 globe : col. ; 12 cm. in diam.
```

4) *Maps, and two-dimensional graphic items (except filmstrips, filmslips, and slides).* Give the height and width in centimetres to the next centimetre up.

```
1 map : col. ; 25 x 35 cm.

1 poster : col. ; 30 x 38 cm.
```

5) *Microfiches.* Give the height and width in centimetres to the next centimetre up, unless they are the standard dimensions (10.5 cm. × 14.8 cm.). In the latter case, do not give the dimensions.

```
3 microfiches ; 12 x 17 cm.
```

6) *Motion pictures and microfilm reels.* Give the gauge (width) in millimetres.

```
1 film reel (12 min.) : sd. ; 16 mm.

1 microfilm reel ; 16 mm.
```

7) *Slides.* Do not give the dimensions if they are 5 × 5 cm.

8) *Sound discs and computer disks.* Give the diameter in inches.

```
1 sound disc : analog, 33 1/3 rpm, stereo. ;
12 in.

1 sound disc (49 min.) : digital, stereo. ;
4 3/4 in.

1 computer disk : 5 1/4 in.
```

9) *Three-dimensional objects.* Give the height, *or* the height and width, *or* the height, width, and depth (as appropriate) in centimetres.

```
1 sculpture : marble ; 110 cm. high

1 quilt : cotton, red & white ; 278 x 200 cm.
```

If the object is in a container, name the container (for example, "in box") and add the dimensions of the container.

```
1 diorama ; in box 30 x 20 x 17 cm.
```

5E. Accompanying material

5E1. Definition. "Accompanying material" is material issued with, and intended to be used with, the item being catalogued. It is often, but not always, in a different physical form from the item. Examples include: a slide set with an accompanying book; a book with an accompanying atlas; a filmstrip with an accompanying sound recording.

5E2. Give the number of physical units and the name of any significant accompanying material. Use the terms listed in rule 5B when possible.

```
323 p. : ill. ; 24 cm. + 6 maps

3 v. : ill. (some col.) ; 27 cm. + 1 set of
teacher's notes

1 score ; 26 cm. + 1 sound cassette

1 filmstrip : col. ; 35 cm. + 1 sound disc
```

```
1 computer disk ; 5 1/4 in. + 1
demonstration disk
```

If the accompanying material is minor, *either* describe it in a note (see rule 7B10) *or* ignore it.

6. SERIES AREA

Contents:
    6A. Preliminary rule
    6B. Title proper of series
    6C. Statements of responsibility relating to series
    6D. Numbering within series
    6E. Subseries
    6F. More than one series

6A. Preliminary rule

6A1. Punctuation
Precede this area by a full stop, space, dash, space (. —).
Enclose each series statement in parentheses (()).
Precede a statement of responsibility relating to a series by a space, diagonal slash, space (/).
Precede the numbering within a series by a space, semicolon, space (;).
Precede the title of a subseries by a full stop, space (.).

6A2. Sources of information. Take information recorded in this area from the item itself or its container. Do not give series information taken from any other source.

6B. Title proper of series

6B1. Transcribe the title proper of the series as found on the item or its container. See rule 1B for instructions on how to record titles proper.

```
(About Britain . . . [8]

(Penguin crime fiction . . .

(Family library of great music . . .
```

8. The three dots here and in the other examples in rule 6 indicate that other elements (for example, numbering) may be necessary to complete the series statement.

6B2. If more than one form of the series title is found on the item and its container, give the form found on the item itself. If more than one form appears on the item or if the variant forms appear only on the container, give the form that best identifies the series.

> (Carrier cookery cards . . .
> (*appears on the item as:* Cookery cards *and as* Carrier cookery cards)

6C. Statements of responsibility relating to series

Only give statements of responsibility about persons or corporate bodies responsible for the series if they appear on the item or its container *and* if they are necessary to identify the series. See rule 1F for instructions on how to record statements of responsibility.

> (Works / Thomas Hardy . . .

> (Sound cassettes / Institute for the New Age . . .

Do not record statements relating to editors of series.

> (Society and the Victorians . . .
> *not*   (Society and the Victorians / general editor John Spiers . . .

6D. Numbering within series

6D1. Give the numbering or other designation of the item within the series if that numbering appears on the item or its container. Give the numbering or other designation in the terms in which it appears (for example, if a numbering appears as roman numerals, give roman numerals). Use standard abbreviations (for example, use "no." for "number" and "v." for "volume").

> (Collectors pieces ; 14)

> (VideoClassics ; 312)

> (Family library of great music ; album 5)

> (Sounds of the seventies ; no. 54)

> (Polyphony ; v. E)

> (Art and the modern world ; 1981A)

6E. Subseries

If the item is part of a series that is itself part of a larger series *and* both series are named on the item or its container, give the details of the larger series before the details of the smaller series.

```
(Science. The world environment)

(Music for today. Series 2 ; no. 8)
```

6F. More than one series

If the item belongs to two or more separate series *and* both are named on the item or its container, give the details of each series separately. Give the series statements in the order in which they appear on the item.

```
(Video marvels ; no. 33) (Educational
progress series ; no. 3)
```

7. NOTE AREA

Contents:
  7A. Preliminary rule
  7B. Notes

7A. Preliminary rule

7A1. Give useful descriptive information that cannot be fitted into the rest of the description in a note. A general outline of types of notes is given in rule 7B. If a note seems to be useful, give it even if it is not in that general outline. When appropriate, combine two or more notes to make one note.

7A2. Punctuation

Precede each note by a full stop, space, dash, space (. —) *or* give each note as a separate paragraph (see rule 0D).

Separate any introductory word(s) of a note (for example, "Contents", "Summary") from the rest of the note by a colon, space (:).

7A3. Sources of information. Take notes from any suitable source.

7A4. Form of notes

Order. Give notes (if there is more than one note) in the order in which they are given in the general outline (see rule 7B).

References to other works. When referring to another work, give those of the following elements that are relevant:

> Title / statement of responsibility.
> Edition. Place : publisher, date.

Give them in that order and with that punctuation.

> Revision of: Understand the law / J.P.
> Smith. 3rd ed.

> Originally published: London : Jamptons &
> Hardwycke, 1888

> Facsimile reprint of: New ed., with
> additions. Oxford : Printed for R. Clements,
> 1756

Formal notes. Use formal notes (those with the same introductory word(s)) if they can be easily understood and if they save space.

Informal notes. When writing your own notes, make them as brief and clear as possible.

7B. Notes

7B1. Special notes for serials and computer files.
Frequency. If the item being described is a serial, give the frequency of issue as the first note unless the frequency is obvious from the title (for example, "Annual report", "Monthly digest").

> Annual

> Weekly

> Issued every month except August

> Six issues yearly

> Irregular

Note changes in frequency.

> Weekly (1968-1981), monthly (1982-   )

System requirements. Always make a System requirements note when describing a computer file. Give the make and model of the computer(s) on which it will run *and* any other system requirements

40

that are important to its use (for example, amount of memory, peripherals). Precede the note with "System requirements:".

> System requirements: Apple family

> System requirements: IBM PC or 100% compatible; 64K; colour monitor

> System requirements: IBM PC XT or AT; CD-ROM player and drive

7B2. Nature of the item. Make a note giving the nature, scope, or artistic form of the item if it is not obvious from the rest of the description.

> Documentary

> Comedy in two acts

> Original recordings from 1921 to 1933

7B3. Language. Make a note on the language(s) of the item if it is not obvious from the rest of the description.

> Commentary in English

> French dialogue, English subtitles

7B4. Adaptation. If the item is a manifestation of a work that is an adaptation of another work, make a note about the other work.

> Based on short stories by P.G. Wodehouse

> Spanish version of: Brushing away tooth decay

> Translation of: Dona Flor e seus dois maridos

7B5. Titles. Make notes on important titles borne by the item that are different from the title proper.

> Title on container: Butterflies and moths

> Disc 3 entitled: This amazing world

If the title of a serial varies slightly, say so.

> Title varies slightly

If each issue of a serial has an individual title, say so.

Each issue has its own title

If you have supplied the title from other than the chief source of information, indicate the source.

Title taken from: List of Chicago jazz recordings, 1940-1950 / B. McEnroe

Title from script

7B6. Credits and other statements of responsibility.
Cast. List featured players, performers, narrators, or presenters.

Presenter: Wallace Greenslade

Cast: Diane Keaton, Woody Allen, Michael Murphy, Mariel Hemingway, Karen Ludwig, Meryl Streep

Credits. List persons (other than the cast) who have made an important contribution to the artistic or technical production of a motion picture, sound recording, videorecording, etc., *and* are not named in the statements of responsibility.

Credits: Producer, Peter Rogers; director, Gerald Thomas

Credits: Guitar and vocals, Eric Clapton; keyboards, Dick Sims; vocals, Marcy Levy; guitar, Georgy Terry; bass guitar, Carl Radle; drums, Jamie Oldaker

Backing by the Amazing Lost Cowboys

Piano: Gerald Moore

Other statements of responsibility. Give the names of any person(s) or body (bodies) not named in the statement of responsibility that has an important connection with the item.

Attributed to Aubrey Beardsley

Based on music by Fats Waller

7B7. Edition and history. If the item is a revision or reissue, make a note about the earlier item.

Formerly available as: Those rockin' years

    Reprint of the August 30th 1938 issue

    Rev. ed. of: The portable Dorothy Parker

Serials. Make a note linking the serial being described to another serial if it is continued by or continues another serial
or is supplementary to another serial
or has any other significant relationship to another serial.

    Continued by: The Irish history newsletter

    Continues: Bird watcher's gazette

    Supplement to: The daily collegian

    Absorbed: New society, 1988

7B8. Publication, etc. Give important details of the publication or distribution of the item that cannot be given in the publication, etc., area.

    Distributed in Canada by: West Coast
    Enterprises

7B9. Physical details. Give important physical details that cannot be given in the physical description area.

    Magnetic sound track

    In two containers

    Collage of wood, fabric, & paper

    Unmounted

    Pattern: Fannie's fan

7B10. Accompanying material and supplements. Give important information about accompanying and supplementary material that cannot be given elsewhere in the description.

    Consists of clear plastic model and
    accompanying tape/slide set and instructional
    booklet. 16 p.

    Set includes booklet: The Dada influence.
    32 p.

    Slides with every 7th issue

    Sunday issue includes magazine supplement

7B11. Audience. If the intended audience for the item is not apparent from the rest of the description, state it here.

    Intended audience: Grades 3-5

    For adolescents

    Intended audience: Post-graduate
    engineering students

7B12. Other formats available. Give details of other formats in which the content of the item has been issued.

    Issued also on cassette tape

    Issued also as cassette (VHS or Sony U-
    Matic)

    Issued also for IBM PC and PC-compatible
    hardware

7B13. Summary. Give a brief summary of the content of an item if it is required by the policy of your library.

    Summary: Melissa and her friends discover a
    hidden treasure and defeat a gang that wants
    to steal it

    Summary: Episodes from the novel about a
    corrupt library administrator, read by the
    author

    Summary: A brief historical account of the
    discovery of antibiotics

    Summary: A reading exercise presenting some
    aspects of Native American culture

7B14. Contents. If the item consists of a number of named parts, list those parts in the order in which they occur if the policy of the library requires such listings. Separate the names of the parts by a space, dash, space (—).

    Contents: Polonaise in F sharp minor, op. 44
    -- Polonaise in A flat, op. 53 -- Polonaise in
    A, op. 40, no. 1 -- Nocturne, op. 27, no. 1 --
    Etude, op. 10, no. 3 -- Mazurka in B flat, op.
    7, no. 1

```
Contents: Queen Lucia -- The male
impersonator -- Lucia in London
```

```
Contents: Trent's last case -- Trent's own
case / with H. Warner Allan -- Trent intervenes
```

If the item contains a part that is not evident from the rest of the description, note that here.

```
Includes some poems
```
   (*title is:* Collected prose works)

```
Includes three études and two mazurkas
```
   (*title is:* Chopin's polonaises)

```
Includes bibliographical references
```

7B15. Copy being described, library's holdings, and restrictions on use. Make notes on:

a) important descriptive details of the copy being described

```
Library's set lacks slides 7, 8, and 9
```

```
Library's copy signed by the author
```

b) your library's holdings of an incomplete multipart item

```
Library has issues for 1921 through 1951 and
1953 to date
```

```
Some issues missing
```

c) any restrictions on use of the item.

```
Available to graduate students and faculty
only
```

7B16. "With" notes. If the item being catalogued lacks a collective title *and* the title given in the title and statement of responsibility area applies to only part of that item (see rule 1G) because you are making a separate entry for each of the parts of the item, make a note beginning "With:" and listing the titles of the other parts in the order in which they occur.

```
With: Symphony no. 5 / Beethoven (side B)
```

```
With: Aimless love / J.M. Morgan --
Headwinds / Joe M. Philipson
```

8. STANDARD NUMBER

Contents:
8A. Preliminary rule
8B. Standard number

8A. Preliminary rule

8A1. Punctuation

Precede this area by a full stop, space, dash, space (. —) *or* start a new paragraph (see rule 0D).

8A2. Sources of information. Take standard numbers from any suitable source.

8B. Standard number

8B1. Give the International Standard Book Number (ISBN), or International Standard Serial Number (ISSN), or any other internationally agreed standard number of the item being described. Precede that number with the standard abbreviation (ISBN, ISSN, etc.) and use standard hyphenation.

    ISBN 0-8389-3346-7

    ISSN 0002-9869

8B2. If the item has more than one such number, give the one that applies specifically to the item being described.

    ISBN 0-379-00550-6
    (the ISBN for the set being described; volume 1 also
    carries an ISBN for that volume; but do not record the
    ISBN for the volume)

9. SUPPLEMENTARY ITEMS

9A. Supplementary items described independently.

If a supplementary item has its own title *and* can be used independently, make a separate description. Link it to the item to which it is supplementary by making a note (see rule 7B7).

```
Hye sharzhoom : the newspaper of the
California State University, Fresno
Armenian Students Organization and Armenian
Studies Program. -- Vol. 2, no. 1 (Nov.
1979)-    . -- Fresno : Armenian Studies
Program, CSUF, 1978-
        v. : ill. ; 44 cm.
     Quarterly
     Title also appears in Armenian script
     Vol. 1 consisted of unnumbered "special
issues"
     Supplement to: The daily collegian
```

9B. Supplementary items described dependently.

If a supplementary item has no independent title *or* cannot be used independently:

either record the supplementary item as accompanying material (see rule 5E)

```
        5 v. : ill. ; 32 cm. + 1 v.
```

or make a note (see rule 7B10).

```
Note:  Accompanied by supplement (37 p.) issued in
       1969
```

10. ITEMS MADE UP OF MORE THAN ONE TYPE OF MATERIAL

10A. Apply this rule to items that are made up of two or more parts, two or more of which belong to separate material types (for example, a book and a sound recording).

10B. If the item has a main component, make a description based on that main component and give details of the secondary component(s):

either as accompanying material (see rule 5E)

```
        47 slides : col. + 1 sound tape reel
```

or in a note (see rule 7B10).

```
3 v. : ill. ; 30 cm.
```

Note: Sound disc (12 min. : analog, 45 rpm,
mono. ; 7 in.) in pocket at end of vol. 3

10C. If the item has no one main component, follow the rules below as well as the other rules in this part.

10C1. General material designation. If you are using general material designations (see rule 1C), *and* the item has a collective title, give "[kit]".

```
Multisensory experience for the pre-
schooler [kit]
```

If the item has no collective title, give the appropriate designation after each title.

```
Telling the time [filmstrip].  The story of
time [sound recording]
```

10C2. Physical description. *Either* give separate physical descriptions for each part or group of parts belonging to each distinct class of material, starting a new paragraph with each physical description

```
Tomato growing [kit] : a multimedia
presentation / concept, Dion Garber ;
programmer, Trev Baxter. -- Dallas :
Thraxton Multimedia, 1988
   46 slides : col.
   1 sound disc (15 min.) : analog, 45 rpm,
mono. ; 7 in.
   1 computer disk ; 5 1/4 in.
   (AgriMedia ; A32)
```

or give a general term as the statement of extent for items with a large number of different materials. Add the number of pieces if that number can be ascertained easily.

```
various pieces

36 pieces
```

10C3. Notes. Make notes on each of the particular parts of the item as the first note(s).

```
Tape cassette also available as disc. --
Slides photographed in Death Valley, Calif.
```

11. FACSIMILES, PHOTOCOPIES, AND OTHER REPRODUCTIONS

In describing a facsimile, photocopy, or other reproduction in eye-readable or microform, describe the facsimile, etc., and not the original. Give data relating to the original in a single note.

```
Demos : a story of English socialism /
George Gissing ; edited with an
introduction by Pierre Coustillas. --
Brighton, Sussex : Harvester Press, 1972.
  477 p. ; 23 cm. -- (Society and the
Victorians)
  Facsimile reprint of: New ed. London :
Smith Elder, 1897

Alice's adventures underground / by Lewis
Carroll ; with a new introduction by Martin
Gardner. -- New York : Dover, 1965.
  91 p. : ill. ; 22 cm.
  Complete facsimile of the British Museum
manuscript of: Alice's adventures
underground
```

PART 2

Headings, Uniform Titles, and References

Introduction

When you have made a standard description according to rules 0–11, add access points (name headings and/or titles) in accordance with the rules in this part to that description to create a catalogue entry. The rules that follow deal with the choice of access points (21–29), with their form (30–61), and with the making of references (62–65). General rules precede specific rules. If you cannot find an appropriate specific rule, use the preceding general rule.

The rules in this part apply to all library materials (printed, audiovisual, machine-readable, serial, etc.).

Rules 42–43, 46B, and 51 deal with additions to access points. Always make these additions (if possible) if they are necessary to differentiate between otherwise identical access points in the same catalogue. For example:

```
Robertson, John, 1903-1971

Robertson, John, 1918-
```

If you wish, make such additions if they are not needed now, so that future conflicts can be avoided.

As in rules 0–11, the examples in the following rules are supposed only to illustrate the rule, not to add to it. In cases of doubt, always prefer the rule as guidance rather than the examples.

The presentation of examples is intended to help you to understand the rules. It is not intended to imply a certain form of presentation in your catalogue. The transcriptions from the source of information are set out in ISBD style (see part 1). In a few instances (see, for example, rule 25C2), more information than is required for a standard description is included to demonstrate the rule fully.

Choice of Access Points

Contents

21. INTRODUCTION

21A. Main and added entries

Use rules 23–29 to decide the access points (name headings and/or titles) that are to be added to the bibliographic description (see rules 0–11) so that the description can be added to, and retrieved from, a catalogue.

Use rules 23–28 to decide which access point is the heading for the main entry (other access points being headings for added entries). If, however, your library does not distinguish between main entries and added entries, treat all access points as equal and use rules 23–29 to tell you which and how many access points to make.

Generally, each rule and its example(s) only covers certain added-entry access points. Additional added-entry access points (for example, series and title headings) may be required by the general rule on added entries (see rule 29).

21B. Sources for determining access points

Prefer the chief source of information (see rule 0A) to other sources, but also take into account any relevant information found elsewhere on the item and, when necessary, in reference sources.

21C. Form of examples

The examples in rules 24–29 only indicate the access points to be made without showing their complete form. Use rules 30–61 to establish the complete form.

When an example is followed by "Main entry under title" or "Added entry under title," it usually means the title proper (see rule 1B). In a few cases it may mean the uniform title (see rules 57–61).

22. CHANGES IN TITLES PROPER

22A. Definition

In some instances, make a new catalogue entry for a work if its title changes (see rules 22B and 22C). A title proper has changed if:

1) any word other than an article (for example, "the," "a," "le"), a preposition (for example, "to," "de," "of"), or a conjunction (for example, "and," "but," "aber") is added, deleted, or changed

or

2) there is a change in the order of the first five words (six if the title begins with an article).

However, ignore the change if it is:

1) in the representation of a word or words (for example, ignore a change from "Trout and salmon news" to "Trout & salmon news")
2) after the first five words (six if the first is an article) and does not change the meaning of the title (for example, ignore a change from "The journal of the antiquities of Bootle and surroundings" to "The journal of the antiquities of Bootle and its environs")
3) the addition or deletion of the name of the issuing body at the end of the title (for example, ignore a change from "The journal of the cuisine of provincial Indiana of the League of Hoosier Gourmets" to "The journal of the cuisine of provincial Indiana")

or

4) the addition, deletion, or change of punctuation (for example, ignore a change from "Boot, shoe, sandal news" to "Boot/shoe/sandal news").

22B. Monographs

If the title proper of a monograph in more than one physical part (for example, a multivolume book) changes from one part to another, use the title proper of the first part as the title proper of the whole monograph. Make a note (see rule 7B5) about the other title(s).

```
    The romance of the tomato : a seven part
instructional film / devised and presented
by Gervase Scudamore. -- London : Hamberger
& Pollock, 1987
    7 film cassettes (20 min. each) : sd.,
col. ; standard 8 mm.
    Cassettes 6 and 7 entitled: The tomato
and you
```

54

If, however, a title used in later parts predominates (for example, if volume 1 has one title and volumes 2–9 have another title), use the title proper of the later parts as the title proper of the whole monograph. Make a note (see rule 7B5) about the other title(s).

22C. Serials

If the title proper of a serial changes, make a separate main entry for each title. Link these entries with notes (see rule 7B7).

23. GENERAL RULE

23A. Works of personal authorship

23A1. Definition. A personal author is the person who is chiefly responsible for the content of a work. Examples are:

> writers of books
> composers of music
> artists (sculptors, painters, etc.)
> photographers
> compilers of bibliographies
> cartographers (makers of maps)

In some cases (see rule 27B1g), treat performers as the authors of sound recordings.

23A2. Enter a work by one person under the heading for that person (see rule 24A).

Enter a work by two or more persons under:
the principal personal author (see rule 25B1)
or the person named first (see rules 25B2, 25C1, and 27)
or its title (see rules 25C2 and 26B).

Make added entries as instructed in rule 29.

23B. Entry under corporate body

23B1. Definition. A corporate body is an organization or group of persons that has a name. If you are in doubt as to whether words indicating a particular body constitute a name, treat them as a name if they have initial capital letters *and/or* if they begin with the definite article (for example, "The," "Le"). For example, "The British Museum" is a name and "a group of concerned citizens" is not; "The Modern Jazz Quartet" is a name and "seven rock superstars" is not. In other cases of doubt, do not regard the phrase as a name.

Examples of corporate bodies are:

> business firms
> governments (local and national)
> government agencies (local and national)
> churches
> associations (for example, clubs, societies)
> institutions (for example, museums, libraries)
> international agencies
> conferences
> exhibitions, expeditions, and festivals
> performing groups

Some corporate bodies are subordinate to (part of) other bodies. For example, the Henry Madden Library is a part of the California State University, Fresno; the Home Office is part of the government of the United Kingdom.

23B2. Enter a work issued by a corporate body or originating from a corporate body under the heading for that body (see rule 24B) if it is one or more of the following:

a) an administrative work dealing with:
the corporate body itself (for example, an annual report)
or   its policies, procedures, operations, etc. (for example, a policy statement, a staff manual)
or   its finances (for example, a budget, a financial report)
or   its personnel (for example, a staff list)
or   its resources or possessions (for example, a catalogue, an inventory, a membership directory)
b) a law or collection of laws, an administrative regulation, a treaty (*for detailed guidance on these materials, see the full* AACR2R)
c) a report of a committee, commission, etc. (provided that the report states the opinion of the committee, etc., and does not merely describe a situation objectively)
d) a liturgical text for which a particular church, denomination, etc., is responsible (*for detailed guidance on these materials, see the full* AACR2R)
e) a collection of papers given at a conference (provided that the conference is named prominently in the item being catalogued); the report of an expedition (provided that the expedition is named prominently in the item being catalogued)

56

f) a sound recording, videorecording, or film created *and* performed by a group

g) a map or other cartographic material created as well as published by a corporate body.

If such a work originates from two or more bodies, see also rules 25–27.

If a work does not fall into one of the types listed above, or if you are in doubt about whether it does, enter it under a person's name or under title as appropriate. In addition, make added entries under the names of prominently named corporate bodies as instructed in rule 29B2e.

23C. Entry under title

Enter a work under its title when:

1) the author is unknown *and* no corporate body is responsible (see rule 23B2)

2) the work has more than three authors *and* none of them is the principal author (see rule 25C2) *and* no corporate body is responsible (see rule 23B2)

3) it is a collection *or* a work produced under editorial direction *and* has a collective title (see rule 26B)

4) it is not by a person or persons *and* is issued by a corporate body *but* is not one of the types of publication listed in rule 23B2

5) it is a sacred scripture (such as the Bible, the Koran, or the Talmud) *or* an ancient anonymous work (such as *Beowulf* or the *Arabian nights*).

24. WORKS FOR WHICH ONE PERSON OR CORPORATE BODY IS RESPONSIBLE

24A. Works by one person

Enter a work by one person under the heading for that person even if he or she is not named in the item being catalogued.

> The good soldier / by Ford Madox Ford
> *Main entry under the heading for Ford*

> I.F. Stone's newsletter
> *Main entry under the heading for Stone*

> Wavelength / Van Morrison
> *(a sound recording composed, produced, and performed by Morrison)*
> *Main entry under the heading for Morrison*

57

Don Quixote
  (*a print by Picasso*)
Main entry under the heading for Picasso

Collins Italian gem dictionary :
Italian-English, English-Italian / Isopel
May
Main entry under the heading for May

Newts in the wild : London ponds / made
by Norma McEachern
  (*a filmstrip*)
Main entry under the heading for McEachern

Ecstasy and me : my life as a woman /
Hedy Lamarr
  (*the "ghosted" autobiography of a movie star, "ghost-
  writer" not named*)
Main entry under the heading for Lamarr

Enter a collection of, or selections from, works by one person under the heading for that person even if she or he is not named in the item being catalogued.

The Brandenburg concertos / J.S. Bach
Main entry under the heading for Bach

The poems of John Keats / edited by Jack
Stillinger
Main entry under the heading for Keats

The sweet singer of Penge
  (*a collection of poems published anonymously but
  known to be by Eric Lancaster*)
Main entry under the heading for Lancaster

Selected essays / George Orwell
Main entry under the heading for Orwell

24B. Works for which one corporate body is responsible

If a work originating from a single corporate body falls into one or more of the categories listed in rule 23B2, enter it under the heading for the body.

Entry under corporate heading

Administrative works

> Annual report of the Institute for the
> Furtherance of Psychic Studies
> *Main entry under the heading for the Institute*

> Additions to the Library / H.D. Timpson
> Library, Branksome
> *Main entry under the heading for the Library*

> Rules and regulations of the Chicago
> Board of Trade
> *Main entry under the heading for the Board*

Laws, etc.

> The health and safety at work act 1974
>   (*a British law*)
> *Main entry under the heading for the United Kingdom*

> Rules, regulations, and by-laws relating
> to the storage and sale of fish / City of
> Minneapolis
> *Main entry under the heading for Minneapolis*

Committee, etc., reports

> Report and recommendation to the Governor
> and the General Assembly / Illinois
> Commission on the Status of Women
>   (*a serial*)
> *Main entry under the heading for the Commission*

> Hartford Civic Center Coliseum roof
> collapse : final report / Common Council
> Committee to Investigate the Coliseum Roof
> Failure
> *Main entry under the heading for the Committee*

Liturgical works

> Rite of marriage. -- Washington : United
> States Catholic Conference
> *Main entry under the heading for the Catholic Church*

Conference, etc., proceedings

> Abstracts of the annual meeting / Free
> Thought Society
> *Main entry under the heading for the Society's meeting*

> Proceedings / Conference on the Mass
> Media and the Black Community, Cincinnati,
> 1969 ; sponsored by the Pen and Paper Club
> of Cincinnati
> *Main entry under the heading for the Conference*

Works created and performed by a group

> Exile on Main Street / the Rolling Stones
> *(a sound recording composed, produced, and performed*
> *by the rock group)*
> *Main entry under the heading for the group*

> Free South Africa! : an improvisational
> video performance / the Children of the
> Universe
> *Main entry under the heading for the group*

Maps created and published by a corporate body

> Fresno & Fresno County. -- Modesto, Ca. :
> Compass Maps, 1986
> *Main entry under the heading for Compass Maps*

Entry not under corporate heading

> Italians in America / made and released
> by the Anti-Defamation League of B'nai
> B'rith
> *(a filmstrip)*
> *Main entry under title*
> *Added entry under the heading for the League*

> Symphony no. 8 in B minor (Unfinished) /
> Schubert
> *(a sound recording by the Philadelphia Orchestra)*
> *Main entry under the heading for Schubert*
> *Added entry under the heading for the Orchestra*

> Bulletin / Pinner Ornithological Society
> *Main entry under title*
> *Added entry under the heading for the Society*

60

California library directory : listings
for public, academic, special, state
agency, and county law libraries / Library
Development Services Bureau, California
State Library
Main entry under title
Added entry under the heading for the Bureau

Costs and revenue of national newspapers
/ National Board for Prices and Incomes
Main entry under title
Added entry under the heading for the Board

Near Eastern art in Chicago collections /
the Art Institute of Chicago, November 17,
1973-January 20, 1974
(*a catalogue of an exhibition*)
Main entry under title
Added entry under the heading for the Institute

25. WORKS FOR WHICH TWO OR MORE PERSONS OR CORPORATE BODIES ARE RESPONSIBLE

25A. Scope
Apply this rule to:

1) works produced by two or more persons (joint authors, collaborators, etc.)
2) works for which two or more persons have prepared separate contributions (including the records of debates and discussions)
3) works consisting of letters, etc., exchanged by two or more persons
4) works issued by, or originating from, two or more corporate bodies *and* that fall into one or more of the categories listed in rule 23B2.

For works produced by two or more persons directed by an editor, see rule 26.

For works consisting of collections of, or selections from, already existing works (such as anthologies), see rule 26.

For special types of collaboration, see rule 27.

25B. Principal responsibility indicated

25B1. If the layout or wording of the chief source of information of a work by two or more persons or bodies indicates clearly that one person or body is chiefly responsible, enter under the heading for that person or body. Make added entries under the headings for the other persons or bodies if there are not more than two of them.

> The Taylor system in Franklin management :
> application and results / by George D.
> Babcock in collaboration with Reginald
> Trautschold
> *Main entry under the heading for Babcock*
> *Added entry under the heading for Trautschold*

> Unknown horizons : visions of the distant
> future : a video experience / Maude LaFarge
> with the help of Simon, Paul, and Janette
> *Main entry under the heading for LaFarge*

> Technical services in libraries :
> acquisitions, cataloging, classification,
> binding, photographic reproduction, and
> circulation operations / by Maurice F.
> Tauber and associates
>   (*the seven associates are named on the leaf following*
>   *the title leaf*)
> *Main entry under the heading for Tauber*

25B2. If two or three persons or bodies are shown as being principally responsible, enter under the heading for the one named first. Make added entries under the headings for the others.

> Elementary differential equations with
> linear algebra / Ross L. Finney, Donald R.
> Ostberg with the assistance of Robert G.
> Kuller
> *Main entry under the heading for Finney*
> *Added entry under the heading for Ostberg*

25C. Principal responsibility not indicated

25C1. If, in a work by two or three persons or bodies, no one person or body is clearly principally responsible (see rule 25B), enter under the heading for the one named first. Make added entries under the headings for the others.

Women artists, the twentieth century /
authors Karen Petersen, J.J. Wilson
(*a slide set*)
Main entry under the heading for Petersen
Added entry under the heading for Wilson

The basement tapes / Bob Dylan & the Band
(*sound recording of songs written and performed by
Dylan and the rock group the Band*)
Main entry under the heading for Dylan
Added entry under the heading for the Band

General college mathematics / W.L. Ayres,
Cleota G. Fry, H.F.S. Jonah
Main entry under the heading for Ayres
Added entries under the headings for Fry and Jonah

25C2. If, in a work by four or more persons or bodies, none of the persons or bodies is clearly principally responsible (see rule 25B), enter under title. Make an added entry under the heading for the first person or body named in the chief source of information.

Outlaw country / Willie Nelson, Waylon
Jennings, David Allan Coe, Hank Williams, Jr.
(*sound recording; all four performers named on the
labels*)
Main entry under title
Added entry under the heading for Nelson

The art of Gauguin / Richard Brettell,
Françoise Cachin, Claire Fréches-Thory,
Charles F. Stuckey
(*exhibition catalogue; all four authors named on title
page*)
Main entry under title
Added entry under the heading for Brettell

26. COLLECTIONS AND WORKS PRODUCED UNDER EDITORIAL DIRECTION

26A. Scope
Apply this rule to:

1) collections of independent works, or extracts from individual works, by different persons or bodies (for example, anthologies)
2) works consisting of contributions by different persons or bodies acting under editorial direction (for example, some encyclopaedias and textbooks)

3) works that are combinations of 1 and 2, above.

Do not apply this rule to works covered by rule 23B2 (for example, conference proceedings).

26B. With collective title

If an item belongs to one of the types listed in rule 26A *and* has its own collective title, enter it under that title.

If the item has one, two, or three editors or compilers named in the chief source of information, make added entries under the headings for each of them. If there are four or more editors or compilers named in the chief source of information, make an added entry under the heading for the one named first.

> The new Oxford book of English light verse /
> chosen by Kingsley Amis
> *Main entry under title*
> *Added entry under the heading for Amis*

> The modern age / edited by Boris Ford
> (*essays by various people produced under the editorship
> of Ford*)
> *Main entry under title*
> *Added entry under the heading for Ford*

> The family of man . . . / created by
> Edward Steichen
> (*collection of 503 photographs by various people*)
> *Main entry under title*
> *Added entry under the heading for Steichen*

> Why a duck? : visual and verbal gems from
> the Marx Brothers movies / edited by
> Richard J. Anobile
> *Main entry under title*
> *Added entry under the heading for Anobile*

> The New York times atlas of the world
> ("editorial direction Barry Winkleman, Paul
> Middleton"—*back of the title leaf*)
> *Main entry under title*

26C. Without collective title

If an item belongs to one of the types listed in rule 26A *and* has no collective title, enter it under the heading for the first work or contribution named in the chief source of information. If the item lacks a chief source of information, enter it under the heading for the first work or contribution in the item.

Make added entries under the headings for editors, compilers, and/or contributors as instructed in rule 26B.

> A John Field suite / Harty. A dance in the
> sunshine / Bax. A Shropshire lad, etc. /
> Butterworth. There is a willow grows aslant
> a brook / Bridge
> *Main entry under the heading for Harty*
> *Added entries (name/title; see rule 29B4) under the headings*
> *for Bax, Butterworth, and Bridge*

27. WORKS OF MIXED RESPONSIBILITY

27A. Scope

A work of mixed responsibility is one that involves the collaboration of two or more persons or bodies (see rule 23B2 for cases in which a corporate body is responsible) *and* to which the persons and/or bodies make different kinds of contribution. Examples of the different kinds of contribution are: writing, adapting, illustrating, editing, arranging, translating, performing.

Typical instances of mixed responsibility are:

> a work with text by one person and illustrations by another
> a work created by one person and adapted by another
> a work by one person with a commentary by another
> a work by one person translated by another
> a law for which a corporate body is responsible with a commentary by a person
> a musical work by one person arranged by another
> a musical work by one person performed by another person or by a performing group.

This rule divides all cases of mixed responsibility into two types. These are:

1) modifications of existing works (see rule 27B)
2) new works produced by the collaboration of different persons and/ or bodies making different intellectual or artistic contributions (see rule 27C).

27B. Modifications of existing works

27B1. Enter a work that is a modification of an existing work under the heading for the new work and make a name/title added entry (see rule

65

29B4) for the original work *if* the nature and content of the original has been changed substantially *or if* the medium of expression has changed. Examples of such change are:

a) paraphrases, rewritings, adaptations for children, and versions in a different literary form of written works

> Jump! : the adventures of Brer Rabbit / by Joel Chandler Harris ; adapted by Van Dyke Parks and Malcolm Jones
>> (*adaptation of Harris's* Adventures of Brer Rabbit)
>> *Main entry under the heading for Parks*
>> *Added entry under the heading for Jones*
>> *Added entry (name/title) under the heading for Harris*

> Robert Fitzgerald reads from his Iliad
>> (*sound recording, read by the poet, of his modern version of Homer's* Iliad)
>> *Main entry under the heading for Fitzgerald*
>> *Added entry (name/title) under the heading for Homer*

b) revisions of texts when the reviser(s) is named in the chief source *and* the original author(s) *either* is no longer named in the title and statement of responsibility area *or* is named only in the title proper

> The law of Ireland / G. Fenn
>> ("a complete revision of Innes and Montgomery's Irish law"—*title page*)
>> *Main entry under the heading for Fenn*
>> *Added entries (name/title) under the headings for Innes and Montgomery*

> Roget's Thesaurus of English words and phrases. -- New ed. / completely revised and modernized by Robert A. Dutch
>> *Main entry under the heading for Dutch*
>> *Added entry under the heading for Roget*

c) commentaries when the item is presented as a commentary

> The Theaetetus of Plato : a commentary / by Spenser Sayers
>> (*contains the Greek text of the* Theaetetus)
>> *Main entry under the heading for Sayers*
>> *Added entry (name/title) under the heading for Plato*

66

d) adaptations of graphic art works from one medium of the graphic arts to another

> Courbet's The painter's studio / an
> engraving by M.M.C.
> *Main entry under the heading for M.M.C.*
> *Added entry (name/title) under the heading for Courbet*

e) reproductions of art works with text when the writer of the text is represented as the author of the work in the chief source of information

> William Morris wallpapers and chintzes /
> Fiona Clark
> > (*reproductions of Morris's designs with an annotated*
> > *catalogue by Clark*)
> *Main entry under the heading for Clark*
> *Added entry under the heading for Morris*

f) alterations (free transcriptions, etc.), paraphrases, and variations of musical works

> Rhapsody on a theme by Paganini : for piano
> and orchestra / Rachmaninov
> *Main entry under the heading for Rachmaninov*
> *Added entry under the heading for Paganini*

g) sound recordings of works by different persons performed by a principal performer or performers[1]

> Contrary to ordinary / Jerry Jeff Walker
> > (*ten songs, each by a different composer, performed by*
> > *Walker*)
> *Main entry under the heading for Walker*

> James Galway plays Song of the seashore
> and other melodies of Japan
> > (*compositions by various Japanese composers*
> > *performed by Galway*)
> *Main entry under the heading for Galway*

---

1. Consider such a sound recording to have a principal performer or principal performers when the wording, layout, typography, etc., of the chief source of information or the container clearly present the activity of the performer(s) as the major purpose of the recording.

```
The fine art of surfacing / The Boomtown
Rats
```
    ·   *(songs, by various individual members of the band,*
       performed by a rock group)
    Main entry under the heading for the Boomtown Rats

h) novels, etc., based on motion pictures, television shows, etc.

```
Star wars : the novel of the smash hit movie
/ by E.B. Knowles
```
Main entry under the heading for Knowles
Added entry under the heading for the motion picture

```
The laugh was on Lazarus : a novel based
on the ABC television series The avengers /
John Garforth
```
Main entry under the heading for Garforth
Added entry under the heading for the television series

i) motion pictures, television shows, etc., based on novels, etc.

```
The charmer / by Allan Prior
```
    (six-part television play based on Patrick Hamilton's
      novel Mr. Stimpson and Mr. Gorse)
    Main entry under the heading for Prior
    Added entry (name/title) under the heading for Hamilton

27B2. Enter any other modification of an existing work under the heading for the original work.

Examples of modifications entered under the headings for the original works are:

a) musical works by one person performed by another

```
Willie Nelson sings Kris Kristofferson
```
    (songs by Kristofferson performed by Nelson)
    Main entry under the heading for Kristofferson
    Added entry under the heading for Nelson

b) translations

```
Twenty love poems and a song of despair /
Pablo Neruda ; translated by W.S. Merwin
```
Main entry under the heading for Neruda
Added entry under the heading for Merwin (see rule 29B6)

> True history ; and Lucius, or, The ass /
> Lucian ; translated from the Greek by Paul
> Turner
> *Main entry under the heading for Lucian*
> *Added entry (name/title; see rule 29B8) under the heading*
>   *for Lucian for* Lucius, or, The ass
> *Added entry under the heading for Turner (see rule 29B6)*

c) arrangements of musical works

> Original motion picture soundtrack, The
> sting / featuring the music of Scott Joplin ;
> adapted and arranged by Marvin Hamlisch
> *Main entry under the heading for Joplin*
> *Added entry under the heading for Hamlisch*

d) texts with commentary when the item is presented as an edition of
the text

> Plato's Republic : with a commentary / by
> Roderick Wolfe
> *Main entry under the heading for Plato*
> *Added entry under the heading for Wolfe*

e) abridgements of, and excerpts from, existing works

> Great scenes from Pickwick
>   (*excerpts from Dickens's* Pickwick papers)
> *Main entry under the heading for Dickens*

> My life with Sherlock Holmes :
> conversations in Baker Street / edited by
> J.R. Hamilton
>   (*selections from Sir Arthur Conan Doyle's Sherlock*
>   *Holmes stories*)
> *Main entry under the heading for Doyle*
> *Added entry under the heading for Hamilton*

f) illustrated works.

> The world of Pooh : the complete Winnie-the-
> Pooh and The house at Pooh Corner / by A.A.
> Milne ; with decorations and new
> illustrations in full colour by E.H. Shepard
> *Main entry under the heading for Milne*
> *Added entry under the heading for Shepard (see rule 29B6)*

69

27C. New works produced by persons or bodies making different intellectual or artistic contributions

Enter a work produced by two or more persons or bodies making different intellectual or artistic contributions under the heading for the person or body given prominence by the wording or layout of the chief source of information of the item being catalogued. If there are two or three collaborating persons or bodies, make an added entry under the heading(s) for the other(s).

If no one person or body is given prominence, *and* there are two or three persons or bodies named, enter under the heading for the person or body named first in the chief source. Make an added entry under the heading(s) for the other(s).

If no one person or body is given prominence, *and* there are more than three persons or bodies named, enter under title. Make an added entry under the heading for the person or body named first.

Examples of such collaborative works are:

1) works produced by collaboration between an artist and a writer

> Goodbye baby & amen : a saraband for the
> sixties / David Bailey & Peter Evans
> (*photographs by Bailey, text by Evans*)
> *Main entry under the heading for Bailey*
> *Added entry under the heading for Evans*

2) works produced by collaboration between a composer and a librettist.

> Curlew river : a parable for church
> performance / by William Plomer ; set to music
> by Benjamin Britten
> *Main entry under the heading for Plomer*
> *Added entry under the heading for Britten*

28. RELATED WORKS

28A. Scope

Apply this rule to a separately catalogued work that has a relationship to another separately catalogued work.

Typical examples of related works are:

> continuations and sequels
> supplements
> indexes

concordances
screenplays, scenarios, etc.
subseries
special numbers of serials

For adaptations, revisions, translations, etc., see rule 27.

28B. Enter a related work under its own heading according to the rules on entry (rules 23–27). Make the appropriate added entries according to those rules and rule 29.

Make an added entry under the name heading *or* name/title (see rule 29B4) *or* title, as appropriate, of the work to which it is related.

> Colonel Sun / Robert Markham
>> (*a sequel to Ian Fleming's series of James Bond novels*)
> *Main entry under the heading for Markham*
> *Added entry under the heading for Fleming*

> Index of characters and events in the Pickwick papers / Nigel Appleby
>> (*an index to the novel by Dickens*)
> *Main entry under the heading for Appleby*
> *Added entry (name/title) under the heading for Dickens*

> Blue / writers, Meade Roberts, Ronald M. Cohen
>> (*the screenplay of the motion picture* Blue)
> *Main entry under the heading for Roberts*
> *Added entries under the headings for Cohen and the motion picture*

> English art, 1970 : a special number of Eclectic art review
> *Main entry under title*
> *Added entry under* Eclectic art review

> Writing for love or money : thirty-five essays reprinted from the Saturday review of literature
> *Main entry under title*
> *Added entry under* Saturday review of literature

> Carleton journalism review
>> (*distributed with* Content : Canada's national news media magazine)
> *Main entry under title*
> *Added entry under* Content

29. ADDED ENTRIES

29A. General rule

29A1. Scope. Rule 29 gives general guidance on the making of added entries. Use it to supplement the specific instructions in rules 23–28.

29A2. Make an added entry under the heading for a person or corporate body or under a title if some users of the catalogue might look under that heading or title rather than under the main entry heading. If in doubt as to whether to make an added entry, make it.

29A3. Construct a heading for an added entry according to the instructions in rules 30–61.

For instructions on name/title added entry headings, see rule 29B4.

29A4. If the reason for an added entry is not apparent from the description (for example, if a person or body used as the basis for an added entry heading is not named in a statement of responsibility or in the publication details), make a note giving the name of the person or body (see rule 7B6) or the title (see rule 7B4).

29B. Specific applications

29B1. Two or more persons or corporate bodies involved. If the following subrules and examples refer to only one person or body, and two or three persons or bodies are involved in the work which you are cataloguing, make added entries under the headings for each.

If four or more persons or bodies are involved in a particular instance, make an added entry under the heading for the one named first in the chief source of information of the item being catalogued.

29B2. Examples of added entries. Typical examples of name added entries are:

a) collaborators

> The basement tapes / Bob Dylan & the Band
> (*songs written and performed by Dylan and the rock group the Band*)
> *Main entry under the heading for Dylan*
> *Added entry under the heading for the Band*

Captions courageous, or, Comments from the gallery / by Bob Reisner and Hal Kapplow

Main entry under the heading for Reisner
Added entry under the heading for Kapplow

Banned books 287 B.C. to 1978 A.D. . . . / by Anne Lyon Haight ; updated and enlarged by Chandler B. Grannis

Main entry under the heading for Haight
Added entry under the heading for Grannis

The Oxford book of wild flowers / illustrations by B.E. Nicholson ; text by S. Ary & M. Gregory

Main entry under the heading for Nicholson
Added entries under the headings for Ary and Gregory

Roman and pre-Roman glass in the Royal Ontario Museum : a catalogue / John W. Hayes

Main entry under the heading for the Museum (see rule 23B2)
Added entry under the heading for Hayes

b) editors, compilers, revisers, etc.

The Penguin book of animal verse / introduced and edited by George MacBeth

Main entry under title
Added entry under the heading for MacBeth

The Oxford book of light verse / chosen by W.H. Auden

Main entry under title
Added entry under the heading for Auden

The novels of Jane Austen / the text based on collation of the early editions by G.W. Chapman

Main entry under the heading for Austen
Added entry under the heading for Chapman

73

c) original authors

> Hoyle's rules of games . . . / edited by
> Albert H. Morehead and Geoffrey Mott-Smith
> *Main entry under the heading for Morehead*
> *Added entry (name/title; see rule 29B4) under the heading*
> *for Hoyle*
> *Added entry under the heading for Mott-Smith*

> The new Roget's thesaurus of the English
> language in dictionary form / by Norman
> Lewis
> *Main entry under the heading for Lewis*
> *Added entry (name/title; see rule 29B4) under the heading*
> *for Roget*

d) performers

> James Galway plays Mozart
>   (*accompanied by the London Symphony Orchestra*)
> *Main entry under the heading for Mozart*
> *Added entries under the headings for Galway and the*
> *Orchestra*

> To Lefty from Willie
>   (*sound recording of Lefty Frizzell's songs performed by*
>   *Willie Nelson*)
> *Main entry under the heading for Frizzell*
> *Added entry under the heading for Nelson*

e) corporate bodies with responsibility beyond that of publishing.

> A field guide to the birds . . . / text and
> illustrations by Roger Tory Peterson. -- 2nd
> rev. and enl. ed. / sponsored by the National
> Audubon Society
> *Main entry under the heading for Peterson*
> *Added entry under the heading for the Society*

> Desalination : a tape/slide presentation
> / Creative Media, Inc. for the Desalination
> Company
> *Main entry under title*
> *Added entries under the headings for the two companies*

74

Fifty years of modern art, 1916-1966 /
Edward B. Henning. -- Cleveland : Cleveland
Museum of Art
    (catalogue of a loan exhibition)
Main entry under the heading for Henning
Added entry under the heading for the Museum

Sex and the Californian / Present Topics,
Inc.
    (a videorecording)
Main entry under title
Added entry under the heading for Present Topics

The Paris Commune of 1871 / by Frank
Jellinek
    (a "Left Book Club edition")
Main entry under the heading for Jellinek
Added entry under the heading for the Club

Closing the catalog : proceedings of the
1978 and 1979 Library and Information
Technology Association institutes
Main entry under title
Added entry under the heading for the Association

Hampstead past and present / issued with
the approval of the Hampstead Borough
Council
Main entry under title
Added entry under the heading for the Council

29B3. Other related persons or bodies. If the heading will provide an important access point, make an added entry under the heading for any person or body that has a relationship to a work not covered in rules 23–28 or in the preceding parts of rule 29.

A short title catalogue of the Warren N. and
Suzanne B. Cordell collection of dictionaries
. . .
    (catalogue of a special collection held by the
    Cunningham Library, Indiana State University)
Main entry under the heading for the Library
Added entries under the headings for W.N. and S.B. Cordell

```
Currents in anthropology : essays in
honor of Sol Tax / edited by Robert Hinshaw
```
Main entry under title
Added entries under the headings for Tax and Hinshaw

29B4. Related works. Make an added entry under the main entry heading for a work to which the work being catalogued is closely related (see rules 26C, 27, and 28 for guidance in specific cases).

Make such entries in the form of the heading for the person or corporate body or title under which the related work is, or would be, entered. If the heading is for a person or corporate body, *and* the title of the related work differs from the title of the work being catalogued, add the title of the related work to the heading to form a name/title added entry heading.

```
Gore Vidal's Caligula : a novel based on
Gore Vidal's original screenplay / by William
Howard
```
Main entry under the heading for Howard
Added entry under the heading for the motion picture
    Caligula
Added entry (name/title) under the heading for Vidal

```
The long riders : original motion picture
sound track / music composed and arranged
by Ry Cooder
```
Main entry under the heading for Cooder
Added entry under the heading for the motion picture The
    long riders

If appropriate, substitute a uniform title (see rules 57–61) for a title proper in a name/title or title added entry heading.

```
Adventures of Tom Sawyer / by Mark Twain
; rewritten for young readers by Felix
Sutton
```
Main entry under the heading for Sutton
Added entry (name/title) under the heading for Twain
    followed by the uniform title Tom Sawyer

29B5. Titles. Make an added entry under the title proper of every item entered under a personal heading, a corporate heading, or a uniform title unless:

a) the title proper is essentially the same as the main entry heading or a reference to that heading

> Metropolitan Museum of Art : the official
> guide
> *Main entry under the heading for the Museum*
> *No title added entry*

or

b) the title proper has been composed by the cataloguer.

> [Photograph of Little Richard] / Julia
> Barrett
> *Main entry under the heading for Barrett*
> *No title added entry*

Make an added entry also for any other title (cover title, caption title, running title, etc.) if it is significantly different from the title proper. For guidance on which differences are significant, see rule 22A.

> Dental model / H.J. Brandon
> (*title on container:* Elementary dental work)
> *Main entry under the heading for Brandon*
> *Added entries under title proper and* Elementary dental
> work

29B6. Special rules for translators and illustrators

a) *Translators.* If the main entry is under the heading for a corporate body *or* under a title, make an added entry under the heading for a translator.

> Proceedings of the 6th Annual Conference of
> Italian School Administrators / translated by
> L. Del Vecchio
> *Main entry under the heading for the Conference*
> *Added entry under the heading for Del Vecchio*

> The New Testament . . . : a translation
> . . . / by Ronald A. Knox
> *Main entry under the heading for the* New Testament
> *Added entry under the heading for Knox*

If the main entry is under the heading for a person, make an added entry under the heading for the translator if:

i) the translation is in verse

> The sonnets of Michelangelo / translated by
> Elizabeth Jennings
> *Main entry under the heading for Michelangelo*
> *Added entry under the heading for Jennings*

or   ii) the work has been translated into the same language more than
once

> The betrothed (I promessi sposi) : a
> Milanese story of the seventeenth century /
> by Alessandro Manzoni ; translated by Daniel
> J. O'Connor
>> (*one of a number of English translations of* I promessi
>> sposi)
> *Main entry under the heading for Manzoni*
> *Added entry under the heading for O'Connor*

or   iii) the wording of the chief source of information implies that the
translator is the author.

> Thumbelina / Anne Smythe
>> (*a translation of H.C. Andersen's* Tommelise)
> *Main entry under the heading for Andersen*
> *Added entry under the heading for Smythe*

b) *Illustrators.* Make an added entry under the heading for an illustrator
if:

i) in the chief source of information, the illustrator's name is given
equal prominence with, or more prominence than, the name of
the person or body used in the main entry heading

> Insects : a guide to familiar American
> insects / by Herbert S. Zim and Clarence
> Cottam ; illustrated by James Gordon Irving
>> (*all names given in the same size of type*)
> *Main entry under the heading for Zim*
> *Added entries under the headings for Cottam and Irving*

or   ii) the illustrations occupy half or more of the item

> Hans Christian Andersen's The nightingale /
> designed and illustrated by Nancy Ekholm Burkert
>> (*Burkert's name not given equal prominence; the*
>> *illustrations occupy more than half of the volume*)
>> *Main entry under the heading for Andersen*
>> *Added entry under the heading for Burkert*

or   iii) the illustrations are considered to be an important part of the work.

> Handley Cross / by the author of Mr.
> Sponge's sporting tour ; with seventeen
> coloured illustrations and one hundred
> woodcuts by John Leech
>> (*Leech's name not given equal prominence; most of the*
>> *book is text; Leech is one of the most famous Victorian*
>> *book illustrators*)
>> *Main entry under the heading for the author (Surtees)*
>> *Added entry under the heading for Leech*

29B7. Series. Make an added entry under the heading for a series for each separately catalogued item in the series *if* the added entry provides a useful grouping of entries. *Optionally,* add the numeric or other designation of each work in the series.

> The natural history of Selborne / Gilbert
> White . . . (The world's classics ; no. 22)
> *Main entry under the heading for White*
> *Added entry under:* World's classics *or* World's
> classics ; no. 22

> Piano concerto no. 2 in B flat, op. 83 /
> Brahms . . . (Family library of great
> music ; album 4)
> *Main entry under the heading for Brahms*
> *Added entry under:* Family library of great music *or* Family
> library of great music ; album 4

> Kitagawa Utamaro (1753-1806) / text by
> Ichitaro Kondo ; English adaptation by
> Charles S. Terry . . . (Library of Japanese
> art ; no. 5)
> *Main entry under the heading for Kondo*
> *Added entry under:* Library of Japanese art *or* Library of
> Japanese art ; no. 5

```
The golden key / by George MacDonald ;
with pictures by Maurice Sendak . . . (A
yearling book)
```
Main entry under the heading for MacDonald
Added entry under: Yearling books

```
International distribution of catalogue
cards : present situation and future
prospects / R.S. Giljarevskij . . . (Unesco
manuals for libraries ; 15)
```
Main entry under the heading for Giljarevskij
Added entry under: Unesco manuals for libraries *or* Unesco
manuals for libraries ; 15

```
Books do furnish a room : a novel /
Anthony Powell . . . (The music of time /
Anthony Powell ; 10)
```
Main entry under the heading for Powell
Added entry under: Powell, Anthony. Music of time *or*
Powell, Anthony. Music of time ; 10

29B8. Analytical added entries. An analytical entry is an entry for:
a separately titled section of a work
or
a separate work contained in a collection.
Make analytical entries as required by your library's policy.
Two methods of making analytical entries are given here. Choose the
most appropriate for the item that you are cataloguing.

a) *Name/title added entry headings.* Make an analytical entry by using
the name/title or title heading of the part as an added entry heading.

```
Melville, Herman
   Billy Budd
   Great short novels ; an anthology / by
Edward Weeks. -- New York : Literary Guild
of America, c1941
   999 p. ; 26 cm.
   Contains twelve short novels by English
and American writers
```

b) *"In" entries.* If you require more detail in the analytical entry, make
an *"In"* entry. Such entries consist of:

80

For the part

    the name/title or title heading
    the title proper and statement(s) of responsibility (see rule 1)

and, if relevant,

    the edition statement (see rule 2)
    the publication, etc., details (see rule 4)
    the extent, other physical details, dimensions (see rule 5)
    notes (see rule 7)

the word *In*
and, *for the whole item*

    the name/title *or* title heading
    the title proper and statement(s) of responsibility (see rule 1)

and, if relevant,

    the edition statement (see rule 2)
    the publication, etc., details (see rule 4).

```
Eliot, George
  The lifted veil / George Eliot. -- p.
198-246 ; 26 cm.
  In Eliot, George. Silas Marner ; The
lifted veil ; Brother Jacob. -- London :
Oxford University Press, 1906

Dickens, Charles
  A Christmas carol / by Charles Dickens. --
p. 171-234 : ill. (some col.) ; 24 cm.
  In Once upon a time : the fairy tale
world of Arthur Rackham. -- London :
Heinemann, 1972

Tolkien, J.R.R.
  Guide to the names in the Lord of the
rings / J.R.R. Tolkien. -- p. 168-216 ; 20
cm.
  In A Tolkien compass / edited by Jared
Lobdell. -- New York : Ballantine, 1980
```

Headings for Persons

ADDITIONS TO DISTINGUISH IDENTICAL NAMES

42. ADDITIONS TO NAMES CONTAINING, OR CONSISTING OF, INITIALS

43. DATES

30. INTRODUCTION

In making a heading for a person, take the following three steps.

First, choose the name that will be the basis for the heading. Most persons are only known by one name. In some cases, however, a person is identified by two or more names *or* by two or more forms of the same name. For example, the same woman is known as *Jacqueline Kennedy* and *Jacqueline Onassis*, and the same man is known as *Herblock* and *Herbert Block*.

Second, decide which part of the chosen name should be the first word in the heading (the "filing element"). Again, in the majority of cases this is simply the surname. In some cases, however, the choice is not so obvious. For example, should it be *Gaulle, Charles de* or *De Gaulle, Charles*?

Third, make references from different names for the same person or from different parts of the chosen name. For example, you should refer from *Geisel, Theodore* to *Seuss, Dr.*; from *Clay, Cassius* to *Ali, Muhammad*; and from *Da Vinci, Leonardo* and *Vinci, Leonardo da* to *Leonardo, da Vinci*.

Rules 31–44 deal with the first two steps and with their associated problems. Rule 63 deals with the third.

CHOICE OF NAME

31. GENERAL RULE

31A. Choose, as the basis for the heading, the name by which a person is commonly known. It may be the person's real name, pseudonym, nickname, title, name in religion, initials, or any other type of name. For persons using pseudonyms, see also rule 32A.

31B. Apply the following subrules to decide the form of name by which a person is commonly known.

31B1. Names containing surnames.[2] If a person is identified by a name that contains a surname:

a) use the form of name that appears in the chief sources of information (see rule 0A) of works by that person in his or her language

        Clara Jones

        Willie Nelson

        Lester Del Rey

        Elinor M. Brent-Dyer

        Studs Terkel

        D.H. Lawrence
not   David Herbert Lawrence

        P.G. Wodehouse
not   Pelham Grenville Wodehouse
not   Sir Pelham Wodehouse

        Morris West
            (*form of name most commonly found in chief sources*)
not   Morris L. West
            (*form of name found occasionally*)

        Bertrand Russell
not   Bertrand, third Earl Russell

        Sebastien Japrisot
            (*pseudonym*)
not   Jean-Baptiste Rossi
            (*real name*)

        George Eliot
            (*pseudonym*)
not   Mary Ann Evans
            (*name before marriage*)
not   Mary Ann Cross
            (*married name*)

        Duke Ellington
not   Edward Kennedy Ellington

---

2. "Surname," as used in these rules, includes any name used as a family name.

b) if the chief sources of information are of little or no help (as, for example, with painters, sculptors, and choreographers), *or* if the person is not primarily known as a creator of works (as, for example, with politicians and motion picture actors), use the form found in reference sources, other books, and articles issued in the person's language or country.

> Ben Nicholson
>   (*painter*)
>
> Aristide Maillol
>   (*sculptor*)
>
> Okumura Masanobu
>   (*print maker*)
>
> Kirk Douglas
>   (*film star*)
>
> *not*   Issur Danielovitch Demsky
>   (*real name*)
>
> Rita Hayworth
>   (*film star*)
>
> *not*   Margarita Carmen Cansino
>   (*real name*)
>
> Harry S. Truman
>
> Jimmy Carter
>
> *not*   James Earl Carter

31B2. Names not containing surnames. If a person is identified by a name that does not contain a surname:

a) use the name by which he or she is identified in English-language reference sources

> Pope John XXIII
>
> *not*   Joannes Papa XXIII
>
> Saint Ignatius
>
> *not*   San Ignacio
>
> Confucius
>
> *not*   K'ung-tzu
>
> Horace
>
> *not*   Quintus Horatius Flaccus

```
        Alexander the Great
not     Alexandros ho Megas

        Saint Joan of Arc
not     Sainte Jeanne d'Arc

        White Antelope
          (Cheyenne chief)

        Queen Elizabeth II
```

b) if you cannot find the name in English-language reference sources available to you, use the form of name that appears in the chief sources of information (see rule 0A) of works by that person in his or her language.

```
        A.E.
          (pseudonym)
not     George William Russell
          (real name)

        Howling Wolf
          (blues singer)

        Herblock
not     Herbert Block

        Ximenes
          (crossword puzzle setter)
not     Derek Macnutt
          (real name)
```

31C. Include any titles of royalty, nobility, or terms of honour (see also rule 40) that usually appear as part of the name.

```
        Dame Wendy Hiller

        Duchess of Windsor

        Lady Jane Grey
```

31D. If the name contains a surname, omit terms (other than those of royalty, nobility, or honour, see rule 31C) that appear with the name.

```
        Karen Schmidt
not     Doctor Karen Schmidt

        Jane Lavelle
not     Lieutenant Jane Lavelle
```

If the name does not contain a surname *or* if it consists of only a surname and a word or phrase, include any terms that normally appear as part of the name.

```
Sister Mary Hilary

Thomas the Rhymer

Geoffrey of Monmouth

Brother Antoninus

Grandma Moses

Dr. Seuss
```

32. CHOICE AMONG DIFFERENT NAMES

32A. Persons using pseudonyms

32A1. One pseudonym. If all the works by a person appear under one pseudonym, choose the pseudonym. Make a reference (see rule 63A) from the real name if you know it.

	Martin Ross
not	Violet Frances Martin
	Henry Green
not	Henry York
	Woody Allen
not	Allen Stewart Konigsberg
	Bryher
not	Anne Winifred Ellerman (*name before marriage*)
not	Anne Winifred McAlmon (*married name*)
not	Anne Winifred Macpherson (*married name*)

If two or more collaborators use a single pseudonym, choose that pseudonym. Make references from the names of the collaborators if they are known.

```
Emma Lathen
```
  (*pseudonym of Mary J. Latis and Martha Hennisart*)

32A2. More than one pseudonym. If a person uses more than one pseudonym *or* his or her real name and a pseudonym *and* if the person has
> *either* established separate bibliographic identities (that is, has published groups of similar works under one name and groups of similar works under one or more other names)
>
> *or* is a contemporary author

choose, as the basis for the heading for each work, the name found in the chief sources of information of publications of that work. Make references (see rule 63B) to connect the names.

> ```
> Lewis Carroll
> Charles Lutwidge Dodgson
> ```
> *(separate bibliographic identities)*
>
> ```
> Rampling, Anne
> Rice, Anne
> Roquelaure, A.M.
> ```
> *(pseudonyms used by the same person)*
>
> ```
> Molly Keane
> ```
> *(real name used in some works)*
> ```
> M.J. Farrell
> ```
> *(pseudonym used in some works)*
>
> ```
> Denys Watkins-Pitchford
> ```
> *(real name used in some works)*
> ```
> BB
> ```
> *(pseudonym used in some works)*
>
> ```
> Gore Vidal
> ```
> *(real name used in most works)*
> ```
> Edgar Box
> ```
> *(pseudonym used in some works)*

If different names for such a person appear in different editions of the same work *or* if two or more names appear in the same edition, choose (in this order of preference):
> the name that has most frequently appeared in editions of the work
> the name appearing in the latest edition of the work.

> ```
> Terror by day / by John Creasey writing
> as Gordon Ashe
> ```
> *(all previous editions published as: by Gordon Ashe)*
> *Choose* Gordon Ashe *as the basis for the heading for this work*

```
Belinda / Anne Rice writing as Anne
Rampling
```
(*one earlier edition published as:* by Anne Rampling)
Choose Anne Rice *as the basis for the heading for this work*

If a person using more than one pseudonym *or* his or her real name and a pseudonym:
neither has established separate bibliographic identities
nor is a contemporary author
choose the name by which that person has come to be identified in later editions of his or her works, in critical works, and/or in reference sources.

```
      William Makepeace Thackeray
not   Michael Angelo Titmarsh
not   Mr. Yellowplush
```

32B. Persons not using pseudonyms

If a person, other than one using one or more pseudonyms (see rule 32A), is known by more than one name *or* more than one form of a name, choose the name or form of name (if there is one) by which the person is clearly most commonly known (see rule 31B).

Otherwise, choose (in this order of preference):

1) the name that appears most frequently in issues of the person's works
2) the name that appears most frequently in current reference sources
3) the latest name.

```
      Gerald R. Ford
not   Gerald R. Gardner
not   Leslie King
          (earlier names)

      Bob Hope
not   Leslie Townes Hope
          (real name)

      Jacqueline Onassis
not   Jacqueline Bouvier
not   Jacqueline Kennedy
          (earlier names)

      W.H. Auden
not   Wystan Hugh Auden

      Tony Benn
not   Anthony Wedgewood Benn
          (fuller form)
not   Lord Stansgate
          (disclaimed peerage)
```

```
        Muhammad Ali
not     Cassius Clay
           (earlier name)

        Alicia Markova
not     Alice Marks
           (earlier name)

        Anton Dolin
not     Patrick Healey-Kay
           (earlier name)
```

ENTRY ELEMENT

33. GENERAL RULE

If a person's name (chosen in accordance with rules 31 and 32) consists of more than one part, choose one of the parts as the entry element (the part under which the heading is filed and/or by which it is retrieved). Choose the entry element by following rules 34–39.

33A. Order of elements

33A1. If the entry element is the first part of the name, enter the name in direct order.

```
        Ram Gopal
```

33A2. If the entry element is not the first part of the name, transfer the parts that precede it to follow the entry element. Follow the entry element by a comma.

```
        Ronstadt, Linda
           (name: Linda Ronstadt)

        Procter, Adelaide Ann
           (name: Adelaide Ann Procter)

        Griffith-Joyner, Florence
           (name: Florence Griffith-Joyner)
```

33A3. If the entry element is the proper name in a title of nobility, see rule 35.

```
        Winchilsea, Anne Finch, Countess of
           (name: Anne Finch, Countess of Winchilsea)
```

34. ENTRY UNDER SURNAME

34A. General rule

Enter a name containing a surname[3] under the surname unless the name is to be entered under a title of nobility (see rule 35).

> Fonda, Jane
>
> Harris, Emmy-Lou
>
> Gorman, R.C.
>
> Waters, Muddy

34B. Part of the name treated as a surname

If the name does not contain a surname but contains an element that identifies the person and functions as a surname, enter under that element.

> X, Laura

34C. Compound surnames

34C1. Preliminary rule. Apply the following subrules to names that contain, or appear to contain, compound surnames (those consisting of two or more proper names). Apply the subrules in the order in which they appear.

34C2. Hyphenated surnames. If the parts of the compound surname are usually or sometimes hyphenated, enter under the first element of the compound surname.

> Williams-Ellis, Amabel
>
> Ffrangcon-Davis, Gwen

34C3. Unhyphenated surnames. Some married women. Apply this rule to the names of married women with unhyphenated surnames consisting of the surname before marriage and the husband's surname.

Enter under the first element of the surname if the woman's language is Czech, Hungarian, Italian, or Spanish.

> Bonacci Brunamonti, Alinda
>   (*Italian*)

---

3. "Surname," as used in these rules, includes any name used as a family name.

Enter under the husband's surname if the woman's language is other than those listed above.

> Wilder, Laura Ingalls
> (*American, English speaker*)

> Larsson, Inger Olson
> (*Swedish*)

34C4. Unhyphenated surnames. Others. Enter under the first element of the compound surname unless the person's language is Portuguese.

> Johnson Smith, Geoffrey

> Strauss und Torney, Lulu

but

> Silva, Ovidio Saraiva de Carvalho e
> (*Portuguese*)

34C5. Nature of surname uncertain. If the name appears to contain a compound surname but you are not sure:

a) enter under the last part of the name if the person's language is English or one of the Scandinavian languages

> Robertson, E. Arnot

> Jenkins, Florence Foster

b) enter under the first part of the apparent compound surname if the person's language is neither English nor one of the Scandinavian languages.

> Gonzalez Valdés, Selene

34D. Surnames with separately written prefixes

34D1. Articles and prepositions. If the surname includes an article (for example, "le") *or* a preposition (for example, "van") *or* a combination of the two (for example, "de la," "della"), enter under the part of the surname that is most commonly used as the entry element in listings in the person's language or country of residence. See the list of languages and language groups below. For languages not included in this list, see the full *AACR2R*.

If a person has used two or more languages, enter the name according to (in order of preference):

a) the rule for the language of most of his or her works
b) the rule for English (if English is one of the languages)
c) the rule for the language of the country of his or her residence
d) the rule for the language of the name.

Languages and language groups

English. Enter under the prefix.

>   De Mornay, Rebecca
>
>   De la Rue, Elaine
>
>   L'Amour, Louis
>
>   Le Gallienne, Eva
>
>   Du Bois, Cora Alice
>
>   Van Alstyne, Carol
>
>   Von Braun, Wernher

French. If the prefix consists of an article (for example, "le") or of a contraction of an article and a preposition (for example, "du"), enter under the prefix.

>   Le Bordays, Christiane
>
>   Du Guillet, Pernette
>
>   Des Rosiers, Rachel

Otherwise enter under the part of the name following the preposition.

>   Graffigny, Françoise de
>
>   La Bois, Ghislaine de

German. If the prefix consists of an article or of a contraction of an article and a preposition (for example, "Vom"), enter under the prefix.

>   Am Ende, Eva
>
>   Zum Wald-Mertens, Wera

Otherwise enter under the part of the name following the prefix.

>   Goethe, Johann Wolfgang von
>
>   Beethoven, Ludwig van

Italian. Enter a modern name under the prefix.

    D'Amato, Nicola

    Da Caprile, Nello

    Dell'Arte, Antonietta

For mediaeval and early modern names, see the full *AACR2R*.

Spanish. If the prefix consists of an article only, enter under it.

    Las Heras, Elvira

Enter all other names under the part following the prefix.

    Casas, Bartolome de las

34D2. Other prefixes. If the prefix is not an article, *or* preposition, *or* a combination of the two, enter under the prefix.

    Abu Jaber, Kamel

    Ap Rhys, Angharad

    Ben Gurion, David

    O'Casey, Sean

    FitzGerald, Mary

    Ní Chuilleanáin, Eiléan

35. ENTRY UNDER TITLE OF NOBILITY

35A. Definition

A person of modern times identified by a title of nobility has a name that consists of:

    forename(s)—for example: Anne; George Gordon
    surname—for example: Finch; Byron
    title—for example: Countess of Winchilsea; Baron Byron

Consider those persons who *either* use their titles rather than their surnames in their works *or* are listed under their titles in reference sources[4] to be commonly identified by their titles.

---

4. Disregard reference sources that list members of the nobility *either* all under title *or* all under surname.

35B. General rule

If a person is commonly identified by a title, enter under the proper name in his or her title of nobility. Follow the proper name by the person's forename(s) and surname (in that order) and by the term of rank[5] in the person's language.

> Byron, George Gordon Byron, Baron
> (*name appears in his works as:* Lord Byron)

> Nairne, Carolina Nairne, Baroness
> (*name appears in her works as:* Baroness Nairne *or* Lady Nairne)

> Pompadour, Antoinette Poisson, marquise de
> (*name appears in reference works as:* Madame de Pompadour)

> Russell of Liverpool, Edward Frederick Langley Russell, Baron
> (*name appears in his works as:* Lord Russell of Liverpool)

Enter a person with a title who is not commonly identified by his or her title under surname (see rules 34 and 40) *or* given name (see rules 36 and 40) as appropriate.

35C. If a person acquires a title of nobility, gives up such a title, *or* acquires a new title of nobility, follow the instructions in rule 32B in choosing the name to be used as the basis for the heading.

> Caradon, Hugh Foot, Baron
> (*previously* Sir Hugh Foot)

> Benn, Tony
> (*previously* Viscount Stansgate; *title given up*)

36. ENTRY UNDER GIVEN NAME, ETC.

Enter a person with a name that does not include a surname *and* who is not commonly identified by a title of nobility under the part of the name under which the person is listed in reference sources. Include in

---

5. The terms of rank in the United Kingdom peerage are Duke, Duchess, Marquess (Marquis), Marchioness, Earl, Countess, Viscount, Viscountess, Baron, and Baroness.

the heading any words or phrases that are usually associated with the
name. Precede such words or phrases by a comma (,).

```
Bryher

Emma, of Rheims

John, the Baptist

White Antelope, Cheyenne chief

Leonardo, da Vinci

Teresa, of Avila, Saint

Mary, Queen of Scots

Mary II, Queen of England and Wales

Margaret, Princess, Countess of Snowdon

John XXIII, Pope
```

37. ENTRY OF ROMAN NAMES

Enter a Roman of classical times (before A.D. 476) under the part of
the name most commonly used as entry element in modern reference
sources.

```
Messalina, Valeria

Cicero, Marcus Tullius
```

38. ENTRY UNDER INITIALS, LETTERS, OR NUMERALS

Enter in direct order a name consisting of initials, letters, or numerals.

```
BB

H.D.

110908
```

39. ENTRY UNDER PHRASE

39A. Enter in direct order a name that consists of a phrase that does not
include a surname (see rule 34) or an element that functions as a surname
(see rule 34B).

```
Dr. X
```

```
Father Time
```

Enter in direct order a name that consists of a forename *and* a word or phrase that is *neither* a title (for example, "Lady") *nor* a term of address (for example, "Aunt").

```
Boy George
```

39B. If a name consists of a phrase that contains a surname, enter under the surname.

```
Moses, Grandma
```

If a name consists of a forename and *either* a title *or* a term of address, enter under the forename.

```
Pierre, Chef
```

```
Emma, Aunt
```

ADDITIONS TO PERSONAL NAMES

40. TITLES OF NOBILITY AND TERMS OF HONOUR AND ADDRESS, ETC.

40A. Titles of nobility

Add, to the name of a nobleman or noblewoman not entered under title (see rule 35), the title of nobility in the person's language *if* the title or part of the title commonly appears with the name in works by the person or in reference sources.[6] In case of doubt, add the title.

```
Orczy, Emmuska, Baroness
```

but

```
Buchan, John
    (title Baron Tweedsmuir not used in most works)
```

40B. British terms of honour

Add the British term of honour "Sir," "Dame," "Lord," or "Lady" if the term commonly appears with the name in works by the person *or* in reference sources (see footnote 6).

If a woman's title is derived from her being the wife of a baronet or knight, add the term after the name.

---

6. Disregard reference sources dealing only with the nobility and gentry.

> Kelly, Marie-Noële, Lady
> > (*wife of a knight*)

In all other cases, add the term before the forename(s).

> Dench, Dame Judi
>
> Tippett, Sir Michael
>
> Cecil, Lord David
>
> Greaves, Lady Rosamund

Omit terms of honour that do not commonly appear with the name.

> Wodehouse, P.G.
> > (*term of honour* Sir *not used in his works*)
>
> Fraser, Antonia
> > (*term of honour* Lady *not used in her works*)

41. ADDITIONS TO NAMES THAT DO NOT APPEAR TO BE NAMES

If the name by which a person is identified does not appear to be the name of a person, add a suitable English designation in parentheses.

> Taj Mahal (Musician)

Additions to Distinguish Identical Names

42. ADDITIONS TO NAMES CONTAINING, OR CONSISTING OF, INITIALS

If the name by which a person is identified contains, or consists of, initials *and* the fuller form is known, add the spelled-out form (in parentheses) if necessary to distinguish between names that are otherwise identical.

> Smith, Joan E. (Joan Elaine)
>
> Smith, Joan E. (Joan Eleanor)
>
> K.M. (Kate Maclellan)
>
> K.M. (Karen Morgan)

43. DATES

Add the years of birth and/or death as the last element of a heading if the heading is otherwise identical to another. Give the dates in the form shown below.

> Smith, Joan, 1924-
>   (*living person*)
>
> Smith, Joan, 1837-1896
>   (*both dates known*)
>
> Smith, Joan, 1837?-1896
>   (*year of birth probably 1837*)
>
> Smith, Joan, b.1825
>   (*year of death unknown*)
>
> Smith, Joan, d.1859
>   (*year of birth unknown*)
>
> Smith, Joan E. (Joan Elaine), 1894-1957
>
> Smith, Joan E. (Joan Elaine), 1941-

44. If *neither* a fuller form of name *nor* dates are available, do not add anything and interfile the headings.

> Andrew, Janet
>   A story of the Indian jungles . . . 1857
>
> Andrew, Janet
>   She was only a gentleman's toy . . . 1904
>
> Andrew, Janet
>   Constructing balsa-wood models . . . 1956

Geographic Names

Contents

45. INTRODUCTION

The names of places are used:

a) to distinguish between corporate bodies with the same name

        Labour Party (Ireland)

        Labour Party (New Zealand)

b) as additions to other corporate names (for example, conferences)

        Conference on the Problems of the Rain Forest
            (1988 : San Francisco, Calif.)

c) often, as headings for governments.

        Denmark

        California

        Tyne and Wear

        Chicago

46. GENERAL RULE

46A. Choice of name
Give the name of a place in the form found in (in this order of preference):
    current English-language gazetteers and atlases
    other current English-language reference sources.

	Denmark
not	Danmark

	Vienna
not	Wien

	Mexico City
not	Ciudad de México

	Switzerland
not	Helvetia
not	Schweiz
not	Suisse
not	Svizzera

Rio de Janeiro

Ciudad Juárez

Amsterdam

Sri Lanka

46B. Additions to geographic names

46B1. No addition. Do not add the name of a larger place to the name of a country

	Monaco
not	Monaco (Europe)

	Peru
not	Peru (South America)

or a state, province, territory, etc., of Australia, Canada, Malaysia, the U.S., the U.S.S.R., or Yugoslavia

	British Columbia
not	British Columbia (Canada)

	Georgia
not	Georgia (U.S.)

or any of the following parts of the British Isles: England, the Republic of Ireland, Northern Ireland, Scotland, Wales, the Isle of Man, the Channel Islands.

46B2. Addition. Add to the name of a place, other than one of those listed above, the name of the appropriate larger place in which it is located. Use standard abbreviations for the names of the larger places.

If the place name is being used as entry element, make the addition in parentheses.

```
Birmingham (Ala.)

Birmingham (England)
```

If the place name is being used as an addition, precede the larger place by a comma.

```
Regents College (London, England)

Conference on Knowledge Science (1987 :
    Chicago, Ill.)
```

Examples of appropriate additions are:

Cities

```
Hyde Park (Chicago, Ill.)
```

States, territories, provinces, etc.

```
Newcastle (N.S.W.)

Vancouver (B.C.)

Vancouver (Wash.)

Paris (Ill.)

Urbana (Ill.)

Urbana (Ohio)

Kiev (Ukraine)
```

Parts of the British Isles

```
Dorset (England)

Glasgow (Scotland)

Bangor (Wales)

Bangor (Northern Ireland)

Waterville (Ireland)
```

Countries

     Formosa (Argentina)

     Lucca (Italy)

     Odense (Denmark)

     Paris (France)

47. CHANGES OF NAME

If the name of the place changes, use the latest name

     Namibia
not   South-West Africa

unless you are referring to the place at a time when it used the earlier name. For example, use "Gold Coast" if you are referring to the place before March 6, 1957, and "Ghana" for the place since that date.

Headings for Corporate Bodies

Contents

48. INTRODUCTION

In making a heading for a corporate body, take as many of the following five steps as are applicable.

104

First, choose the name that will be the basis for the heading.

Most bodies are known by only one name. In some cases, however, a body is identified by two or more names (see rules 49–50).

Second, decide whether the name needs additions to distinguish it from other names (see rule 51).

Third, if the body is a conference, other meeting, exhibition, fair, etc., make the omissions and additions set out in rule 52.

Fourth, if the body is part of another body *or* is an agency of government, decide whether the body is to be entered directly or subordinately (see rules 53–56).

Fifth, make references from different names for the same body or from different parts of the chosen name (see rule 64).

49. GENERAL RULE

49A. Form of heading

Decide the form of name of a corporate body (see rule 23B1) from (in this order of preference):

items issued by the body in its language
reference sources (including books and articles about the body).

If the name contains (*or* consists of) initials, omit or include full stops according to the predominant usage of the body.

49B. Direct or indirect entry

Enter a corporate body directly under its own name *unless* rule 54 provides for entering it under the name of a higher or related body *or* rule 55 provides for entering it under the name of a government.

    A-400 Group

    American Library Association

    California State University, Fresno

    Church of England

    Cleveland Orchestra

    Cowboy Junkies
      (*musical group*)

    F.W. Woolworth Company

```
George Fry & Associates

International Wild Life Conference . . .⁷

Juilliard Quartet

Museum of Modern Art

Oral Roberts University

Royal Automobile Club

Scripture Union

Twentieth Century-Fox

University of Iowa

Valley of Peace Lutheran Church
```

49C. Changes of name

If the name of a corporate body has changed, establish a new heading under the new name for works appearing under that name. Refer from the old heading to the new and from the new heading to the old.

```
Ohio College Library Center
    see also the later heading: OCLC

OCLC
    see also the earlier heading: Ohio
        College Library Center
```

50. VARIANT NAMES

50A. Language

If the body's name appears in different languages, use the official English form if there is one.

```
        Franco-American Historical Society
not     Société historique franco-américaine
```

If there is no official English form, use:
either the form in a language familiar to the users of your catalogue
or, if the body's name is in a language unfamiliar to the users of your catalogue, a translation of the name into English.

---

7. For additions to the names of conferences, see rule 52C.

```
      Japan Productivity Centre
not   Nihon Seisansei Hombu
```

50B. Governments

Use the conventional name of a government[8] as the heading. The conventional name is the geographic name (see rules 45–47) of the area over which the government has jurisdiction.

```
      France
not   République française

      Sweden
not   Konungariket Sverige

      Puerto Rico
not   Commonwealth of Puerto Rico

      Dorset
not   County of Dorset

      Rhode Island
not   Aquidneck Island
not   State of Rhode Island and Providence
         Plantations
```

50C. Other variant names

50C1. If, in the same period of time, a body uses different names in items issued by it, use the name that appears in chief sources of information (see rule 0A) rather than forms found elsewhere.

50C2. If different forms appear in the chief sources of information, use (in this order of preference):

a) the form not linked to other words in the chief source

```
      Champaign County Museum
not   County Museum
         (appears as County Museum in book titles, for
            example, Victorian furniture in the County Museum)
```

b) the predominant form

---

8. "Government," as used in these rules, means any body (national, federal, regional, or local) that has jurisdiction over a particular area: country, state, province, county, city, municipality, etc.

        Pierpont Morgan Library
            (*predominant form*)
not   Morgan Library
            (*occasional form*)

        Association of College and Research
            Libraries
            (*predominant form*)
not   ACRL
            (*occasional form*)

c) the brief form

        AFAS
not   Air Force Aid Society

        AFL-CIO
not   American Federation of Labor and Congress of
            Industrial Organizations

        Unesco
not   United Nations Educational, Scientific, and
            Cultural Organization

d) the latest form.

        Hendon Natural History Association
not   Hendon Naturalists Association
            (*two items issued; the first under* Hendon Naturalists
            Association, *the second under* Hendon Natural History
            Association)

51. ADDITIONS TO CORPORATE NAMES

51A. General rule
If two or more bodies have the same name, make additions as instructed
below in parentheses. Use standard abbreviations for the names of larger
places added to place names.

51B. Names of countries, states, etc.
If the body is identified with a country, state, province, etc., rather than
with a local place, add the name of that country, state, province, etc.

        National Portrait Gallery (Great Britain)[9]

---

9. Although the correct form of the name of this country is "United Kingdom," "Great
Britain" is used throughout the CONCISE AACR2 to conform to current library practice.

National Portrait Gallery (U.S.)

Republican Party (Ill.)

Republican Party (Mo.)

51C. In the case of all other bodies, add, as appropriate:

the name of the local place in which the body is located

Roosevelt Junior High School (Eugene, Or.)

Roosevelt Junior High School (Fresno, Calif.)

Royal Hospital (Chelsea, London)

Royal Hospital (Victoria, B.C.)

United Methodist Church (Urbana, Ill.)

United Methodist Church (Urbana, Ohio)

or the institution in which the body is located

Newman Club (Brooklyn College)

Newman Club (University of Maryland)

or the year of founding or the years of the body's existence

Scientific Society of San Antonio (1892-1894)

Scientific Society of San Antonio (1904-   )

or any other appropriate word or phrase in English.

Church of God (Adventist)

Church of God (Apostolic)

Fresno (Calif.)

Fresno (Calif. : County)

St. James' Church (Manhattan, New York,
    N.Y. : Catholic)

St. James' Church (Manhattan, New York,
    N.Y. : Episcopal)

52. CONFERENCES, CONGRESSES, MEETINGS, ETC.

52A. General rule

Give the name of a conference as it appears in chief sources of information. If different forms of the name of the same conference appear in chief sources of information, see rule 50.

52B. Omissions

Omit words that denote the number, frequency, or year of the conference.

> Symposium on the Pre-Raphaelites
>
> *not* Annual Symposium on the Pre-Raphaelites
>
> Conference on Co-ordination of Galactic
>   Research
>
> *not* Second Conference on Co-ordination of Galactic
>   Research
>
> Workshop on Cataloguing Rules and
>   Principles
>
> *not* 1987 Workshop on Cataloguing Rules and
>   Principles

52C. Additions to individual conference names

Add to the heading for an individual conference:

> its number (if there is one)
> the year in which it was held
> the location (city or institution) in which it was held.

> Conference on the Central Nervous System and
>   Behavior (2nd : 1959 : Princeton
>   University)
>
> Conference on Solid Earth Problems (1970 :
>   Buenos Aires, Argentina)
>
> Colloquium on Law and Ethics (1987 :
>   University of Chicago)
>
> Conference on Third World Debt (2nd : 1988 :
>   Cambridge, Mass.)
>
> Clinic on Library Applications of Data
>   Processing (13th : 1976 : Urbana, Ill.)

52D. Series of conferences

If the heading is for a number of conferences, do not add the number, date, or location to the heading.

SUBORDINATE BODIES[10]

53. SUBORDINATE BODIES ENTERED DIRECTLY

Enter a subordinate body (including a body created or controlled by a government) directly under its own name *unless* it does not have an individualizing name (see rule 54) *or* it is a government agency to be entered under the name of the government (see rule 55).

	Cunningham Memorial Library
not	Indiana State University. Cunningham Memorial Library

	Harvard Medical School
not	Harvard University. Medical School

	Illini Union
not	University of Illinois at Urbana-Champaign. Illini Union

	Library and Information Technology Association
not	American Library Association. Library and Information Technology Association

	Symposium on Protein Metabolism . . .
not	Nutrition Symposium. Symposium on Protein Metabolism

	Humboldt State University
not	California State University. Humboldt Campus

	British Library
not	Great Britain. British Library

	Amtrak
not	United States. Amtrak

---

10. "Subordinate bodies," as used in these rules, include related bodies. A related body is one that, though not an administrative part of a higher body, is closely related to it. Examples of related bodies are: "friends" groups; staff associations; staff clubs.

Canada Institute for Scientific and
Technical Information
not   Canada. Institute for Scientific and
Technical Information

Exmoor National Park
not   Great Britain. Exmoor National Park

University of Montana
not   Montana. University

Dundee Harbour Trust
not   Great Britain. Dundee Harbour Trust

54. SUBORDINATE BODIES ENTERED SUBORDINATELY

Enter a subordinate body (other than a body created or controlled by a government, see rule 55) as a subheading of the higher body if:

the name of the subordinate body includes the whole name of the higher body

American Legion. Auxiliary
(*name:* American Legion Auxiliary)

Friends of the Earth. Camden Friends of the
Earth
(*name:* Camden Friends of the Earth)

OCLC. Illinois OCLC Users Group
(*name:* Illinois OCLC Users Group)

University of Southampton. Mathematical
Society
(*name:* Mathematical Society of the University of
Southampton)

but

BBC Symphony Orchestra
not   British Broadcasting Corporation. Symphony
Orchestra

or the subordinate body has a name that is general in nature.

California State University, Fresno. School
of Arts and Humanities

International Council on Social Welfare.
Canadian Committee

```
Sondley Reference Library. Friends of the
    Library

Arthur Wondley Corporation. Research
    Division

California Home Economics Association.
    Orange District

Dartmouth College. Class of 1980
```

In case of doubt, enter the body directly.

```
        Human Resources Centre (London, England)
 not    Tavistock Institute of Human Relations. Human
        Resources Centre
```

55. GOVERNMENT AGENCIES ENTERED SUBORDINATELY

55A. General rule
Enter the name of a body created or controlled by a government under the heading for that government when it belongs to one or more of the following types.

Type 1. An agency whose name is general in nature.

```
        Vermont. Department of Water Resources

        United States. Division of Wildlife Service

        Canada. Royal Commission on Banking and
            Finance

        Illinois. Environmental Protection Agency
```

In case of doubt, enter the body directly.

```
        National Portrait Gallery (Great Britain)
 not    Great Britain. National Portrait Gallery
```

Type 2. An agency that has no other agency above it (for example, a ministry).

```
        Australia. Ministry of the Interior

        Great Britain. Home Office

        United States. Department of State
```

113

Type 3. A legislative body (for example, a parliament, city council, or state legislature).

> Great Britain. Parliament
>
> United States. Congress
>
> Virginia. General Assembly
>
> San Francisco. Board of Supervisors

Type 4. A court.

> United States. Supreme Court
>
> Great Britain. High Court of Justice
>
> United States. District Court (Delaware)
>
> Queensland. Supreme Court

Type 5. A body that is a major armed service (see also rule 56B).

> Australia. Royal Australian Navy
>
> Great Britain. Army
>
> United States. Marine Corps

Type 6. An embassy, consulate, etc.

> Canada. Embassy (U.S.)
>
> Canada. Embassy (Ireland)
>
> Canada. Consulate (Los Angeles, Calif.)

55B. Government officials

Enter heads of state and other government officials who are not identified with the name of a particular agency as instructed below.

55B1. Sovereigns, presidents, heads of state, etc.

Give the name of the government followed by the name of the office, the dates of incumbency, and the brief name of the person.

> Great Britain. Sovereign (1936-1952 : George
>   VI)
>
> United States. President (1977-1981 : Carter)
>
> California. Governor (1967-1975 : Reagan)

55B2. Other government officials. Give the name of the government followed by the name of the office.

> Canada. Prime Minister
>
> New Zealand. Governor-General
>
> Philadelphia. Mayor

56. DIRECT OR INDIRECT SUBORDINATE ENTRY

56A. General rule

If a subordinate body or government agency to be entered subordinately (see rules 54–55) is part of another subordinately entered body or agency, omit the intervening body or bodies *unless* the heading would not provide adequate identification without them.

> American Library Association. Committee on
> Cataloging--Description and Access
>
> *not* American Library Association. Resources and
> Technical Services Division. Committee on
> Cataloging--Description and Access
>
> *but*
>
> American Library Association. Resources and
> Technical Services Division. Nominating
> Committee
>
> *not* American Library Association. Nominating
> Committee
>
> United States. Office of Human Development
> Services
>
> *not* United States. Department of Health,
> Education, and Welfare. Office of Human
> Development Services
>
> *but*
>
> Great Britain. Department of Employment.
> Personnel Division
>
> *not* Great Britain. Personnel Division

56B. Armed services

If a government agency is part of a major armed service, enter it as a subheading of that major armed service.

Great Britain. Army. Middlesex Regiment

United States. Army. Corps of Engineers

Great Britain. Army. Infantry Regiment, 57th

United States. Navy. Torpedo Squadron 8

Uniform Titles

Contents

57. INTRODUCTION

57A. A uniform title is a title that brings together entries for different publications of the same work, when those publications have different titles proper. Use of uniform titles is *optional* and the need for them will vary from catalogue to catalogue and from work to work.

57B. If the entry is under a name heading, place the uniform title between the name heading and the title proper, and enclose the uniform title in square brackets.

```
Shakespeare, William
  [Hamlet]
  Shakespeare's Hamlet

Shakespeare, William
  [Hamlet]
  The tragedy of Hamlet, Prince of Denmark
```

If there is no name heading, give the uniform title as the heading.

```
Arabian nights
  The book of a thousand nights and a night
```

117

```
Arabian nights
    Stories from the Arabian nights
```

57C. Omit an initial article from a uniform title.

```
        Dickens, Charles
          [Pickwick papers]
```
not
```
        Dickens, Charles
          [The Pickwick papers]

        Hugo, Victor
          [Misérables]
```
not
```
        Hugo, Victor
          [Les misérables]
```

58. GENERAL RULE

58A. Use uniform titles when:

1) you have two or more publications of the same work in your library *and* those publications have different titles

```
        Dickens, Charles
          [Oliver Twist]
        The adventures of Oliver Twist

        Dickens, Charles
          [Oliver Twist]
          Oliver Twist, or, The parish boy's
        progress
```

2) the publication that you are cataloguing has a title that is unlikely to be looked for by the users of your catalogue

```
        Melville, Herman
          [Moby Dick]
        The whaling story from Moby Dick

        Seuss, Dr.
          [Grinch that stole Christmas]
          Dr. Seuss's The grinch that stole
        Christmas
```

118

```
Potter, Beatrix
  [Story of Mrs. Tiggywinkle]
  Die Geschichte von Frau Tiggywinkle
```

3) you are cataloguing an ancient work or a sacred scripture (see rule 59D)

```
Beowulf
  The story of Beowulf
```

```
Talmud
  New edition of the Babylonian Talmud
```

4) you are cataloguing a collection of, or selections from, the works of a person (see rule 60).

58B. Do not use uniform titles for revisions of works, even when those revisions have different titles.

```
Wodehouse, P.G.
  Three men and a maid
```

```
Wodehouse, P.G.
  The girl on the boat
    (a revised edition of Three men and a maid)
```

59. INDIVIDUAL TITLES

59A. If you use a uniform title, choose the title by which the work is best known. Decide this by consulting reference sources (including other catalogues) *and* other publications of the same work. If you are in doubt about which title is the best known, use the earliest title.

59B. Choose a title in the original language, unless you are cataloguing an older work originally written in a nonroman alphabet language (see rule 59C).

```
Dickens, Charles
  [Martin Chuzzlewit]
  The life and adventures of Martin
Chuzzlewit
```

```
Swift, Jonathan
  [Gulliver's travels]
  The travels of Lemuel Gulliver
```

119

```
Mozart, Wolfgang Amadeus
  [Don Giovanni]
  Il dissoluto punito

Hemingway, Ernest
  [Sun also rises]
  Fiesta

Wodehouse, P.G.
  [Right ho, Jeeves]
  Brinkley Manor
    (Brinkley Manor is the American title of the earlier
    British publication Right ho, Jeeves)

Malory, Sir Thomas
  [Morte d'Arthur]
  King Arthur and the knights of the Round
Table

Caesar, Julius
  [De bello Gallico]
  Caesar's Gallic wars
```

59C. Choose for an older work originally written in a nonroman alphabet language (Russian, Greek, Arabic, etc.), the title by which the work is best known in English-language reference sources.

```
Arabian nights
  The book of 1001 nights

Homer
  [Iliad]
  The sacking of Troy

Aristophanes
  [Frogs]
  A literal translation of Aristophanes'
The frogs
```

59D. Sacred scriptures
Use the uniform title "Bible" for the Bible.

```
Bible
  The Holy Bible
```

In cataloguing a part of the Bible, add "N.T." or "O.T." and, if appropriate, the name of the part.

```
Bible. N.T.
  The New Testament of Our Lord and Saviour
Jesus Christ

Bible. N.T. Gospels
  The Gospels of Matthew, Mark, Luke, and
John

Bible. O.T. Genesis
  The book of Genesis
```

For sacred scriptures other than the Bible, use the form of title found in English-language reference sources.

```
Talmud

Avesta

Book of Mormon
```

60. COLLECTIVE TITLES

60A. Complete works
Use the uniform title "Works" for the complete works of a person.

```
Shakespeare, William
  [Works]
  The complete works of Shakespeare

Shakespeare, William
  [Works]
  Shakespeare's works
```

60B. Selections
Use the uniform title "Selections" for selected works, or extracts from works, in more than one form by the same person.

```
Burns, Robert
  [Selections]
  Poems and letters of Robert Burns
```

60C. Works in one form
Use an appropriate uniform title in English for a collection of all the works in one form by one person.

```
Scott, Sir Walter
  [Novels]
  The Waverley novels

Beethoven, Ludwig van
  [Symphonies]
  Beethoven's symphonies
```

61. ADDED ENTRIES AND REFERENCES

61A. Works entered under uniform title

Make an added entry (see rule 29B5) under the title proper of each publication entered under a uniform title.

```
Arabian nights
  The thousand and one nights
```
Added entry under: Thousand and one nights

61B. Works entered under a name heading

Make a reference from the name heading and the title proper, *and* make an added entry under the title proper, of each publication entered under a name heading and a uniform title.

```
United States
  [Constitution]
  Your rugged Constitution
```
Reference from: United States. Your rugged Constitution
Added entry under: Your rugged Constitution

```
Twain, Mark
  [Tom Sawyer]
  The adventures of Tom Sawyer
```
Reference from: Twain, Mark. Adventures of Tom Sawyer
Added entry under: Adventures of Tom Sawyer

```
Scott, Sir Walter
  [Novels]
  The Waverley novels
```
Reference from: Scott, Sir Walter. Waverley novels
Added entry under: Waverley novels

References

62. GENERAL RULE

62A. "See" references

Apply this rule to a person *or* corporate body *or* work when he, she, or it is known by a name *or* form of name that differs from the one used as the heading for that person *or* body *or* as the uniform title for that work.

Make a "see" reference from the variant form to the one used. Do not make a reference, however, if that reference would file in your catalogue so close to the heading as to be unnecessary.

Make additions to variant names as necessary (see rules 40–43, 51, and 52C).

62B. "See also" references

If two headings or titles are closely related, make "see also" references to connect them (see rules 63B, 64B, and 65B).

63. NAMES OF PERSONS

63A. "See" references

63A1. Refer from a name *or* form of name used by a person *or* found in reference sources, if it differs significantly from that used in the heading for that person.

Typical instances are:

Pseudonym to real name

>   Lucas, Victoria
>   see Plath, Sylvia

Real name to pseudonym

>   Montgomery, Bruce
>   see Crispin, Edmund

>   Monroe, Hector Hugh
>   see Saki

Secular name to name in religion

>   Kiernan, Bridget
>   see De Lourdes, Sister

Earlier name to later name

>   Barrett, Elizabeth
>   see Browning, Elizabeth Barrett
>   Bouvier, Jacqueline
>   see Onassis, Jacqueline
>   Kennedy, Jacqueline
>   see Onassis, Jacqueline

Fuller name to briefer name

>   Mozart, Johann Chrysostom Wolfgang Amadeus
>   see Mozart, Wolfgang Amadeus

>   Davies, William Henry
>   see Davies, W.H. (William Henry)

>   Doolittle, Hilda
>   see H.D.

Briefer name to fuller name

>   Embleton, G.A.
>   see Embleton, Gerry

63A2. Refer from elements of a name other than the entry element (see rules 33–39) if a person might be sought under that other element.

Typical instances are:

Different elements of a compound name

> West, Vita Sackville
>   <u>see</u> Sackville-West, Vita

Part of surname following a prefix

> Maurier, Dame Daphne du
>   <u>see</u> Du Maurier, Dame Daphne

Prefix

> De Graffigny, Françoise
>   <u>see</u> Graffigny, Françoise de

Part of a name not containing a surname

> Gopal, Ram
>   <u>see</u> Ram Gopal
>
> Muhammad Ali
>   <u>see</u> Ali, Muhammad

Inverted form of name consisting of initials

> A., N.J.
>   <u>see</u> N.J.A.

Direct form of name

> Dr. Seuss
>   <u>see</u> Seuss, Dr.

63B. "See also" references

If the same person is entered under two or more headings, make "see also" references to connect those headings.

> Stewart, J.I.M.
>   <u>see also</u> Innes, Michael
>
> Innes, Michael
>   <u>see also</u> Stewart, J.I.M.
>
> Hibbert, Eleanor
>   <u>see also</u>
>   Carr, Philippa
>   Holt, Victoria
>   Kellow, Kathleen
>   Plaidy, Jean
>   (*make similar references under each of the other
>   headings*)

64. NAMES OF CORPORATE BODIES

64A. "See" references

64A1. Refer from a name *or* form of name used by a body *or* found in reference sources if it differs from that used in the heading for the body.

Typical instances are:

Different name

> Common Market
>   see European Community

> Quakers
>   see Society of Friends

> United States. State Department
>   see United States. Department of State

Different language

> Croix rouge
>   see Red Cross

Briefer form

> H.M.S.O.
>   see Her Majesty's Stationery Office

> American Red Cross
>   see American National Red Cross

> Gestapo
>   see Germany. Geheime Staatspolizei

Fuller form

> International Business Machines
>   see IBM

> Religious Society of Friends
>   see Society of Friends

> European Atomic Community
>   see Euratom

126

Different spelling

> Rumania
> see Romania

Inverted form of name

> Woolworth (F.W.) Company
> see F.W. Woolworth Company

> Madden (Henry) Library
> see Henry Madden Library

Initials to acronym

> U.N.E.S.C.O.
> see Unesco

64A2. Refer to a name entered directly from the name as a subordinate entry.

> California State University, Fresno. Henry
> Madden Library
> see Henry Madden Library

> American Library Association. Library and
> Information Technology Association
> see Library and Information Technology
> Association

> United States. Amtrak
> see Amtrak

> United States. Tennessee Valley Authority
> see Tennessee Valley Authority

64B. "See also" references

Make "see also" references between independently entered but related corporate bodies. If necessary, explain the relationship in the reference.

> Freemasons
> see also
> Royal and Select Masters
> Scottish Rite (Masonic order)
> (*make similar references under each of the other*
> *headings*)

127

```
Radio Writers Guild
   see also the later heading:
   Writers Guild of America, West

Screen Writers' Guild
   see also the later heading:
   Writers Guild of America, West

Writers Guild of America, West
   see also the earlier headings:
   Radio Writers Guild
   Screen Writers' Guild

England
   see also (for 1536-1705)
   England and Wales
   and (for 1706 to date)
   Great Britain
```
   (*make similar references under each of the other*
   headings)

65. TITLES

65A. "See" references

65A1. Make a "see" reference from the name heading and the title proper of each item to the name heading and the uniform title of the work (see also rule 61).

```
Dickens, Charles
   The personal history of David Copperfield
   see Dickens, Charles
          David Copperfield
```

65A2. Make a "see" reference from variants of the title (other than titles proper of items being catalogued, see rule 61) to the uniform title *or* name heading and uniform title.

```
Thousand and one nights
   see Arabian nights

Alice's adventures in Wonderland
   see Carroll, Lewis
          Alice in Wonderland
```

65A3. Make a "see" reference from the name heading (where applicable) and collective title of a work, the parts of which are catalogued separately, to the heading and title *or* title of each part.

```
Tolkien, J.R.R.
  Lord of the rings. 2, Two towers
  see Tolkien, J.R.R.
        Two towers

Arabian nights. Sindbad the sailor
  see Sindbad the sailor
```

65A4. Make a "see" reference from the title of a part of a work to the heading and/or title of the work catalogued as a whole.

```
Old Testament
  see Bible. O.T.

Pentateuch
  see
  Bible. O.T. Pentateuch
  Bible. O.T. Genesis
  [etc.]
```

65B. "See also" references

Make "see also" references to connect related works (see rule 28).

```
Kerr, Orpheus C.
  The cloven foot
  see also Dickens, Charles
              Edwin Drood
  (the Kerr work is an adaptation of Edwin Drood)
  Added entry under Dickens (see rule 28) makes "see also"
    reference from Dickens unnecessary
```

129

APPENDIX I Capitalization

a. HEADINGS

a1. General rule

Capitalize personal and corporate names used as headings and corporate names used as subheadings in accordance with normal usage in the language. For example, capitalize all nouns, adjectives, and verbs in English names. Always capitalize the first word in a name.

```
John, the Baptist

H.D.

De la Mare, Walter

Beauvoir, Simone de

Physician

Third Order Regular of St. Francis

Société de chimie physique

Ontario. High Court of Justice
```

a2. Additions to headings for persons

Capitalize additions to headings for persons (see rules 40–42) in accordance with normal usage in the language. If the addition is given in parentheses, capitalize the first word of the addition and any proper noun or adjective.

```
Moses, Grandma

Deidier, abbé

Emma, of Rheims

Taj Mahal (Musician)

Smith, Joan E. (Joan Eleanor)
```

a3. Additions to names of corporate bodies

Capitalize the first word of each addition to the name of a corporate body.

```
Bounty (Ship)

Knights Templar (Masonic order)

Fresno (Calif. : County)
```

b. TITLE AND STATEMENT OF RESPONSIBILITY AREA

b1. Title elements (general rule)

Capitalize the first word of a title proper, an alternative title, or a parallel title. Capitalize other words, including the first word of any other title information element, in accordance with normal usage for the language. In English, capitalize only proper nouns and proper adjectives.

```
The perils of Pauline

The 1919/20 Breasted Expedition to the Near
East

Les enfants du paradis

IV informe de gobierno

Shakespeare's The two gentlemen of Verona

Journal of bat studies

Still life with bottle and grapes

The Edinburgh world atlas, or, Advanced
atlas of modern geography

Strassenkarte der Schweiz = Road map of
Switzerland

The greenwood tree : newsletter of the
Somerset and Dorset Family History Society

Quo vadis? : a narrative from the time of
Nero

King Henry the Eighth ; and, The tempest
```

b2. Quoted titles

Capitalize the first word of every title quoted.

```
An interpretation of The ring and the book

Selections from The idylls of the king
```

132

Supplement to The Oxford companion to
Canadian history and literature

b3. Titles preceded by dashes

Do not capitalize the first word of a title if it is preceded by a dash indicating that the beginning of the phrase from which the title was derived has been omitted.

--loved I not honour more

b4. Grammatically independent titles of supplements and sections

If the title proper of a supplement or section consists of two or more parts not linked grammatically, capitalize the first word of the title of the second and any subsequent part.

The Travelling Wilburys. Part one

Ecology. Student handbook

Journal of biosocial science. Supplement

Progress in nuclear energy. Series 2,
Reactors

Glossary

This glossary contains definitions of some of the more important cataloguing terms used in these rules. The terms have been defined only within the context of the rules. For definitions of other terms, consult the full *AACR2R or* standard glossaries of bibliographic and library terms *or* technical dictionaries.

Access point. A name, title, word, or phrase under which a bibliographic record may be searched and identified. *See also* Heading.

Accompanying material. Material issued with, and intended to be used with, the item being catalogued.

Added entry. An entry, other than the main entry, by which an item is represented in a catalogue. *See also* Main entry.

Alternative title. The second part of a title proper that consists of two parts joined by the word *or* or its equivalent in another language (for example, *Crushed violet, or, A servant girl's tale*).

Analytical entry. An entry for a part of an item for the whole of which an entry has also been made.

Anonymous. Of unknown authorship.

Area. A major section of the bibliographic description (see rule 0C). *See also* Element.

Art original. An original work of art.

Atlas. A volume of maps, plates, engravings, tables, etc., with or without descriptive text. An atlas may be an independent publication, or it may have been issued to accompany one or more volumes of text.

Author. The person chiefly responsible for the intellectual or artistic content of a work.

Author/title added entry. See Name/title added entry.

Author/title reference. See Name/title reference.

Catalogue. A list of library materials contained in part of a library's collection, a whole library collection, or the collections of a group of libraries, arranged according to some definite plan.

Chart. An opaque sheet containing graphic or tabular data (for example, a wall chart).

Chief source of information. The source in an item preferred as the source from which data given in the bibliographic description are taken.

Collaborator. A person who works with one or more associates to produce a work. For collaborators who make the same kind of contribution, see rule 25. For collaborators who make different kinds of contribution, as in the case of collaboration between an artist and a writer, see rule 27. *See also* Joint author, Mixed responsibility, Shared responsibility.

Collective title. A title proper for an item containing two or more works.

Coloured illustration. An illustration in two or more colours.

Compiler. A person who produces a collection by putting together material from the works of two or more persons or bodies. *See also* Editor.

Compound surname. A surname consisting of two or more proper names, sometimes connected by a hyphen.

Conference. 1. A meeting for the purpose of discussing and/or acting upon a topic. 2. A legislative or governing meeting of the representatives of a corporate body.

Container. A box, record sleeve, folder, etc., in which an item is issued.

Corporate body. An organization or group of persons that is identified by a particular name (for example, an association, government, government agency, religious body, local church, conference).

Cross-reference. See Reference.

Diorama. A three-dimensional representation of a scene created by placing objects, figures, etc., in front of a two-dimensional background.

Distributor. An agent or agency (other than a publisher) that markets an item.

Edition: Books, etc. All copies of an item produced from essentially the same type image and issued by the same entity.

Edition: Computer files. All copies containing essentially the same content and issued by the same entity.

Edition: Unpublished items. All copies made from the same production (for example, the original and carbon copies of a typescript; the copies of a home-made videotape).

Edition: Other materials. All copies of an item produced from essentially the same master copy and issued by the same entity.

Editor. A person who prepares other people's work for publication. *See also* Compiler.

Element. A word, phrase, or group of characters representing a distinct unit of bibliographic information and forming part of an area of the description. *See also* Area.

Entry. A record of an item in a catalogue. *See also* Heading.

Filing title. See Uniform title.

Filmstrip. A length of film containing a succession of images intended for projection one at a time.

Flash card. A card or other opaque material printed with words, numerals, or pictures and designed for rapid display.

Game. A set of materials designed for play according to rules.

General material designation. A term indicating the broad class of material to which an item belongs (for example, "sound recording"). *See also* Specific material designation.

Globe. A model of a celestial body depicted on the surface of a sphere.

Heading. A name, word, or phrase placed at the head of a catalogue entry to provide an access point. *See also* Access point.

Impression. All copies of an edition of a book, etc., printed at one time. *See also* Reprint.

International Standard Book Number (ISBN). See Standard number.

International Standard Serial Number (ISSN). See Standard number.

Item. 1. An object (book, map, manuscript, sound recording, film, computer file, etc.) or set of objects forming the basis for a single bibliographic description. 2. The physical manifestation of a work.

Joint author. A person with shared responsibility for a work. *See also* Shared responsibility.

Key-title. The unique name assigned to a serial by the International Serials Data System (ISDS). The key-title may be different from the title proper of the serial.

Kit. 1. An item containing two or more categories of material, no one of which is identifiable as being predominant; also called "multimedia item." 2. An item consisting of a package of textual materials (for example, a "lab kit," a set of activity cards).

Main entry. A catalogue entry for which the access point is the main entry heading (see rules 21–28). *See also* Added entry.

Manuscript. A text, musical score, map, etc., that is inscribed, handwritten, typewritten, or printed out from a computer.

Masthead. The statement of title, ownership, editors, etc., of a newspaper or periodical. In the case of newspapers it is often found on the editorial page or at the top of page one. In the case of periodicals, it is often found on the contents page.

Microform. Any medium, transparent or opaque, bearing microimages. Microforms include microfilms, microfiches, micro-opaques, etc.

Microscope slide. A slide holding a minute object to be viewed through a microscope or by a microprojector.

Mixed authorship. See Mixed responsibility.

Mixed responsibility. A work of mixed responsibility is one in which different persons or bodies contribute to the intellectual or artistic content by performing different kinds of activities (for example, adapting or illustrating a work written by another person). *See also* Shared responsibility.

Model. A three-dimensional representation of a real thing.

Monograph. A nonserial item. A monograph can be a one-part item or one that is complete, or intended to be completed, in a stated number of separate parts.

Multimedia item. A kit. *See* Kit, first definition.

Multipart item. A monograph consisting of two or more physical pieces. *See also* Monograph.

Name/title added entry. An added entry with an access point consisting of the name of a person or corporate body and a title.

Name/title reference. A reference in which one or both parts consist of the name of a person or a corporate body and a title.

Other title information. Any title borne by an item other than the title proper, alternative title, or parallel title (for example, a subtitle). Other title information does not include variations on the title (for example, spine titles, sleeve titles).

Parallel title. The title proper in another language and/or script recorded in the title and statement of responsibility area (see rule 1D).

Part. One of the units into which an item has been divided by the author, publisher, or manufacturer.

Personal author. See Author.

Picture. A two-dimensional visual representation accessible to the naked eye. Use as a specific material designation (see rule 5B) when a more specific term (for example, "art original," "photograph") is not appropriate.

Predominant name. The name or form of name of a person or corporate body that appears most frequently in the person's works or works issued by the corporate body *or* in reference sources, in that order of preference.

Pseudonym. A name assumed by an author.

Realia. The general material designation (see rule 1C) for actual objects (artefacts or specimens) as opposed to replicas.

Reference. 1. A "See" reference is a direction from one form of a name or title to another. 2. A "See also" reference is a direction from one access point to another. *See also* Name/title reference.

Reference sources. Publications (not just reference works) from which authoritative information may be obtained.

Related body. A corporate body that has a relation to another body other than that of subordination. Related bodies include those that are founded but not controlled by other bodies; those that provide financial and/or other types of assistance to other bodies, such as "friends" groups; those whose members are also members of other bodies, such as employees' associations and alumni associations.

Reprint. 1. A new printing of a book, etc., made from the original type image. 2. A new edition of a book, etc., with substantially unchanged text.

Romanization. Conversion of words not written in the roman alphabet to roman-alphabet form.

Section (serials). A separately published part of a serial with its own designation.

Serial. A publication in any medium that is issued in successive parts (usually bearing numerical or chronological designations) *and* intended to be continued indefinitely. Serials include periodicals; newspapers; annuals (reports, yearbooks, etc.); the journals, memoirs, proceedings, transactions, etc., of societies; and monographic series.

Series. A group of separate items related to one another by the fact that each item bears, in addition to its own title proper, a collective title applying to the group as a whole.

Shared responsibility. Collaboration between two or more persons or bodies performing the same kind of activity in the creation of the intellectual or artistic content of a work. *See also* Collaborator, Joint author.

Slide. Transparent material, usually held in a mount, on which there is a two-dimensional image and that is designed for use in a projector or viewer.

Specific material designation. A term indicating the special class of material to which an item belongs (for example, "sound disc"). *See also* General material designation.

137

Spine title. The title that appears on the spine of a book.

Standard number. The International Standard Number (ISN) (for example, International Standard Book Number (ISBN), International Standard Serial Number (ISSN), or any other internationally agreed upon number that identifies an item uniquely).

Statement of responsibility. A statement, transcribed from the item being described, relating to authors *or* to corporate bodies issuing the item *or* to persons or corporate bodies responsible for the performance of the content of the item.

Subordinate body. A corporate body that is an administrative part of a larger body.

Subseries. A series within a series.

Subtitle. See Other title information.

Supplement. A separately issued item that brings up-to-date or otherwise continues an already published item.

Supplied title. The title provided by the cataloguer for an item that lacks a title proper.

Technical drawing. A drawing made for use in a technical context (for example, engineering).

Title. A word, phrase, character, or group of characters naming an item or the work of which it is a manifestation.

Title page. A page at or near the beginning of a book, atlas, musical score, etc., bearing the title proper. The title page does not include the page on the back of the title leaf (sometimes called the title page verso).

Title proper. The chief name of an item, including any alternative title but excluding parallel titles and other title information.

Transparency. A sheet of transparent material bearing an image and designed for use with an overhead projector or a light box. It may be mounted in a frame.

Uniform title. The title by which a work that has appeared under varying titles is to be identified for cataloguing purposes.

APPENDIX III Comparative Table of Rule Numbers

This table lists the rules in *AACR2R* that correspond, or correspond most nearly, to the rules in THE CONCISE AACR2, 1988 revision. In Part 1, also consult any correspondingly numbered rules in chapters 2–12. For example, where the reference is to *AACR2R* rule 1.1A1, see also 2.1A1, 3.1A1, etc.

Concise AACR2	AACR2R	Concise AACR2	AACR2R
PART 1	PART I	PART 1	PART I
0A	1.0A, 1.1A2, and .0B rules in chapters 2–12	5B3	2.5B17–2.5B22
		5B4	1.5B5
		5C	1.5C
0B	1.0H	5D	1.5D
0C	1.0B	5E	1.5E
0D	1.0C	6A1	1.6A1
0E	1.0D	6B	1.6B
1A1	1.1A1	6C	1.6E
1B	1.1B	6D	1.6G
1C	1.1C	6E	1.6H
1D	1.1D	6F	1.6J
1E	1.1E	7A2	1.7A1
1F	1.1F	7A3	1.7A2
1G	1.1G	7A4	1.7A3
2A1	1.2A1	7B1	12.7B1 and 9.7B1
2B	1.2B		
2C	1.2C	7B2	1.7B1
3A	12.3	7B3	1.7B2
3B	9.3	7B4	1.7B7
3C	3.3	7B5	1.7B4–1.7B5
3D	5.3	7B6	1.7B6
4A1	1.4A1	7B7	1.7B7
4B	1.4B	7B8	1.7B9
4C	1.4C	7B9	1.7B10
4D	1.4D	7B10	1.7B11
4D4	1.4E	7B11	1.7B14
4E	1.4F	7B12	1.7B16
5A1	1.5A1	7B13	1.7B17
5B	1.5B	7B14	1.7B18
5B2	2.5B1–2.5B16	7B15	1.7B20

139

Concise AACR2	AACR2R
PART 1	PART I
7B16	1.7B21
8A	1.8A
8B	1.8B
9	1.9
10	1.10
11	1.11

Concise AACR2	AACR2R
PART 2	PART II
21A	21.0A
21B	21.0B
21C	21.0C
22A	21.2A
22B	21.2B
22C	21.2C
23A	21.1A and 21.5B–21.5C
23B	21.1B and 21.5B
23C	21.1C and 21.5A
24A	21.4A
24B	21.4B
25A	21.6A
25B	21.6B
25C	21.6C
26A	21.7A
26B	21.7B
26C	21.7C
27A	21.8
27B	21.9–21.23
27C	21.24–21.27
28	21.28
29A	21.29
29B1	21.30A
29B2	21.30B–21.30E
29B3	21.30F
29B4	21.30G
29B5	21.30J
29B6	21.30K
29B7	21.30L
29B8	21.30M and 13.1–13.6

Concise AACR2	AACR2R
PART 2	PART II
30	—
31	22.1
32A	22.2B and 21.6D
32B	22.2A and 22.2C
33	22.4A
33A	22.4B
34A	22.5A
34B	22.5B
34C	22.5C
34D	22.5D–22.5E
35	22.6
36	22.8
37	22.9
38	22.10
39	22.11
40A	22.12A
40B	22.12B
41	22.11A
42	22.18
43	22.17
44	22.20
45	23.1
46	23.2 and 23.4–23.5
47	23.3
48	—
49	24.1
50A	24.3A–24.3B
50B	24.3E and 24.6
50C	24.2, 24.3C–24.3D, and 24.3G
51A	24.4A
51B	24.4C2
51C	24.4C1 and 24.4C3–24.4C9
52A	24.3F
52B	24.7A
52C	24.7B
52D	24.3F2 and 24.7B4
53	24.12

Concise AACR2	AACR2R	Concise AACR2	AACR2R
PART 2	PART II	PART 2	PART II
54	24.13	59D	21.37 and 25.17–
55A	24.18, 24.21–		25.18
	24.23, and	60A	25.8
	24.25	60B	25.9
55B	24.20	60C	25.10
56	24.14 and 24.19	61	25.2E
56B	24.24	62	26.1
57	25.1	63	26.2
58	25.2	64	26.3
59A	25.2A	65	26.4
59B	25.3	Appendix I	Appendix A
59C	25.4	Appendix II	Appendix D

Index

Compiled by K. G. B. BAKEWELL

The index covers the rules and Appendices I and II, but not examples or works cited in any of the rules or appendices. All index entries refer to rule numbers. "App. I" and "App. II" refer to the appendices, which begin on page 131.

As the rules are based upon bibliographic conditions rather than specific cases, kinds of work have been indexed only when actually named in a rule (for example, concordances and other kinds of related works named in rule 28). There is no entry under *Encyclopaedias, Directories,* etc., because they could represent several bibliographic conditions.

The index is arranged according to *ALA Filing Rules* / Filing Committee, Resources and Technical Services Division, American Library Association. — Chicago : ALA, 1980.

Abbreviations used in the index

App.   Appendix
n   footnote

154

Slides (*cont.*)
  dimensions, 5D(7)
  extent, 5B1(i)
  general material designation, 1C1
  maps on, general material
    designation, 1C2
  sets, other physical details, 5C(3)
Societies, *see* Corporate bodies
Sound cartridges, *see* Sound
  recordings
Sound cassettes, *see* Sound
  recordings
Sound channels, number of, sound
  recordings, 5C(6)
Sound discs, *see* Discs; Sound
  recordings
Sound, other physical details, 5C
Sound recordings
  accompanying filmstrips or slide
    sets, 5C(3)
  chief source of information, 0A
  dimensions, 5D(8)
  entry under performing group,
    23B2(f)
  entry under principal performer
    27B1(g)
  extent, 5B1(j)
  general material designation, 1C1
  notes, 7B6
  other physical details, 5C(6)
Sound tape reels, *see* Sound
  recordings
Sources of information (*see also*
  Chief source of information),
  0A
  access points, 21B
  corporate headings, 49A
  edition area, 2A2
  names containing surnames, 31B1
  names not containing surnames,
    31B2
  note area, 7A3
  physical description area, 5A2
  publication, distribution, etc.,
    area, 4A2
  series area, 6A2

several chief sources, 0B
standard number area, 8A2
titles, notes on, 7B5
Sovereigns, 55B1
Space, use of, *see* Punctuation
Spanish married women, 34C3
Spanish surnames with prefixes,
  34D1
Special area
  cartographic materials, 3C
  computer files, 3B
  music, 3D
  serials, 3A
Special numbers of serials, *see*
  Related works
Specific material designation (*see*
  also Extent)
  definition, App. II
Speed, sound recordings, 5C(6)
Spellings, variant, *see* Variant
  spellings
Spine title, definition, App. II
Square brackets, use of
  description (general), 0A
  edition area, 2A2
  general material designation, 1A1
  publication, distribution, etc.,
    area, 4A2, 4D4, 4E2(c)
  statements of responsibility, 1F5
  title and statement of
    responsibility area, 1A1
  title proper, 1B6
  uniform titles, 57B
Staff associations, *see* Related
  corporate bodies; Subordinate
  corporate bodies
Staff clubs, *see* Related corporate
  bodies; Surbordinate corporate
  bodies
Standard number area, 8
Standard numbers, 8B
  definition, App. II
Standard titles, *see* Uniform titles
State legislatures, 55A (type 3)
Statement of extent, 5B
Statement of responsibility, 1F
  as part of title proper, 1B2–1B3

158

Michael Gorman is dean of library services at California State University at Fresno; he was formerly director of general services at the University Library of the University of Illinois at Urbana-Champaign. Gorman is the editor of the *Anglo-American Cataloguing Rules, Second Edition*, and the *Anglo-American Cataloguing Rules, Second Edition, 1988 Revision*.

Composed by Impressions, Inc.
    in Times Roman on a Penta-driven
    Autologic APS-μ5 phototypesetting
    system

Printed on 50-pound Glatfelter B- 31,
    a pH-neutral stock, and bound in
    10-point Permalin Roncote by
    Versa Press, Inc.

The paper used in this publication meets the minimum requirements of American
National Standard for Information Sciences—Permanence of Paper for Printed Library
Materials, ANSI Z39.48-1984. ∞